Aladdin

Aladdin
and other tales from the Arabian Nights

PARRAGON

Aladdin
A Parragon Classic

This edition published in 1994 by Parragon Book Service Ltd.
This edition © 1994 Parragon Book Service Ltd.
Avonbridge Industrial Estate
Atlantic Road, Avonmouth
Bristol BS11 9QD

ISBN 1-85813-716-0

Printed and bound in Great Britain by
BPC Paperbacks Ltd

CONTENTS

Part One – ALADDIN

The Wonderful Lamp

Part Two – SINBAD

CONTENTS

PART ONE

ALADDIN

THE WONDERFUL LAMP

In the capital of one of the large and rich provinces of the kingdom of China there lived a tailor, whose name was Mustapha, so poor, that he could hardly, by his daily labour, maintain himself and his family, which consisted of a wife and son.

His son, who was called Aladdin, had been brought up after a very careless and idle manner, and by that means had contracted many vicious habits. He was wicked, obstinate, and disobedient to his father and mother, who, when he grew up, could not keep him within doors, but he would go out early in the morning, and stay out all day, playing in the streets and public places with little vagabonds of his own age.

When he was old enough to learn a trade, his father, not being able to put him out to any other, took him into his own shop, and showed him how to use his needle; but neither good words nor the fear of chastisement were capable of fixing his attention. All that his father could do to keep him at home to mind his work was in vain; for no sooner was his back turned than Aladdin was gone for that day. Mustapha chastised him, but Aladdin was incorrigible; and his father, to his great grief, was forced to abandon him to his own devices; and was so much troubled at not being able to reclaim

3

him, that he fell into an illness, of which he died in a few months.

The mother of Aladdin, finding that her son would not follow his father's business, shut up the shop, sold off the implements of the trade, and with the money she got for them, and what she could get by spinning cotton, hoped to maintain herself and her son.

Aladdin, who was now no longer restrained by the fear of a father, and who cared so little for his mother that, whenever she chid him, he would fly in her face, gave himself entirely over to dissipation, and was never out of the streets from his companions. This course he followed till he was fifteen years old, without giving his mind to any thing whatever, or the least reflection on what would become of him. Things being thus, as he was one day playing, according to custom, in the street, with his vagabond troop, a stranger passing by stood still to observe him.

This stranger was a famous magician, called the African Magician, as he was a native of Africa, and had been but two days come from thence.

The African magician had observed in Aladdin's countenance something which was absolutely necessary for the execution of the plan he came about; he enquired artfully about his family, who he was, and what was his disposition; and when he had learned all he desired to know, he went up to him, and taking him aside from his comrades, said to him, "Child, was not your father called Mustapha the tailor?"

"Yes, sir," answered Aladdin, "but he has been dead a long time."

At these words the African magician threw his arms

4

about Aladdin's neck, and kissed him several times with tears in his eyes. "Alas! my son," cried the African magician with a sigh, "how can I forbear? I am your uncle; your good father was my own brother. I have been a great many years abroad travelling, and now that I am come home in the hope of seeing him, you tell me he is dead. It is a great grief to me to be deprived of the comfort I expected. But it is some relief that, so far as I can remember him, you are so like him." Then he asked Aladdin, putting his hand into his purse, where his mother lived; and as soon as Aladdin had informed him, he gave him a handful of small money, saying "Go, my son, to your mother, give my love to her, and tell her that I will come and see her to-morrow, if I have time, that I may have the satisfaction of seeing where my good brother lived so long, and ended his days."

As soon as the African magician left his newly-adopted nephew, Aladdin ran to his mother, overjoyed at the money his uncle had given him. "Mother," said he, "have I an uncle?"

"No, child," replied his mother, "you have no uncle on your father's side, or mine."

"I have just now come," answered Aladdin, "from a man who says he is my uncle on my father's side, assuring me that he is his brother. He cried and kissed me when I told him my father was dead; and to show you that what I tell you is the truth," added he, pulling out the money, "see what he has given me; he charged me to give his love to you, and to tell you, if he has any time tomorrow, he will come and pay you a visit, that he may see the house my father lived and died in."

"Indeed, child," replied his mother, "your father had

a brother, but he has been dead a long time, and I never heard of another."

The mother and son talked no more then of the African magician; but the next day Aladdin's uncle found him playing in another part of the town with other children, and embracing him as before, put two pieces of gold into his hand, and said to him, "Carry this, child, to your mother, and tell her that I will come and see her to-night, and bid her get us something for supper; but first show me the house where you live."

After Aladdin had showed the African magician the house, he carried the two pieces of gold to his mother, and when he had told her of his uncle's intentions, she went out and bought provisions. She spent the whole day in preparing the supper; and at night, when it was ready, she said to Aladdin, "Perhaps your uncle knows not how to find our house; go and see, and bring him if you meet with him."

Though Aladdin had showed the magician the house, he was very ready to go, when somebody knocked at the door, which Aladdin immediately opened; and the magician came in loaded with wine, and all sorts of fruit, which he had brought for dessert.

After the African magician had given what he brought into Aladdin's hands, he saluted his mother, and desired her to show him the place where his brother Mustapha used to sit on the sofa; and when she had so done, he presently fell down and kissed it several times, crying out, with tears in his eyes, "My poor brother! how unhappy am I, not to have come soon enough to give you one last embrace!" Aladdin's mother desired him to sit down in the same place, but he would not. "No," said he, "I shall take care how I do that; but give me leave to sit here over against it, that if I am deprived of seeing the master of a family so dear to me, I may at least have the pleasure of seeing the place where he used to sit." Aladdin's mother pressed him no farther, but left him at liberty to sit where he pleased.

When the magician had sat down, he began to enter into conversation with Aladdin's mother: "My good sister," said he, "do not be surprised at your never having seen me all the time you were married to my brother Mustapha, of happy memory. I have been forty years absent from this country, which is my native place, as well as my late brother's; and during that time have travelled into the Indies, Persia, Arabia, Syria, and Egypt, and have resided in the finest towns of those countries; and afterwards crossed over into Africa, where I made a longer stay. At last, as it is natural for a man, how distant soever it may be, to remember his native country, relations, and acquaintances, I was very desirous to see mine again, and to embrace my dear brother; and finding I had strength and courage enough to undertake so long a journey, I immediately made the necessary preparations, and set out. I will not tell you the time it took me, all the obstacles I met with, what fatigues I have endured, to come hither; but nothing ever mortified and afflicted me so much as hearing of my brother's death, for whom I always had a brotherly love and friendship. I observed his features in the face of my nephew, your son, and distinguished him from among a number of children with whom he was at play; he can tell you how I received the most melancholy news that ever reached my ears. But it is a comfort to me to

7

find him again in a son who has his most remarkable features."

The African magician, perceiving that Aladdin's mother began to weep at the remembrance of her husband, changed the conversation, and turning towards Aladdin, asked him his name.

"I am called Aladdin," said he.

"Well, Aladdin," replied the magician, "what business do you follow? Are you of any trade?"

At this question Aladdin hung down his head, and was not a little abashed when his mother made answer, "Aladdin is an idle fellow; his father, when alive, strove all he could to teach him his trade, but could not succeed; and since his death, notwithstanding all I can say to him, he does nothing but idle away his time in the streets, as you saw him, without considering that he is no longer a child; and if you do not make him ashamed of it, and make him leave it off, I despair of his ever coming to any good. He knows that his father left him no fortune, and sees me endeavour to get bread by spinning cotton every day; for my part, I am resolved one of these days to turn him out of doors, and let him provide for himself."

After these words, Aladdin's mother burst into tears; and the magician said, "This is not well, nephew; you must think of helping yourself, and getting your livelihood. There are a great many sorts of trades; consider if you have not a liking for some of them; perhaps you did not like your father's trade, and would prefer another: come, do not disguise your feelings from me; I will endeavour to help you." But finding that Aladdin returned no answer, "If you have no mind," continued he, "to learn any trade and prove an honest man, I will take a shop for you, and furnish it with all sorts of fine stuffs and linens, and set you to trade with them; and the money you make of them lay out in fresh goods, and then you will live in an honourable way. Tell me freely what you think of it: you shall always find me ready to keep my word."

This proposal greatly flattered Aladdin, who mortally hated work, and had sense enough to know that such shops were very much esteemed and frequented, and the owners honoured and respected. He told the magician he had a greater liking for that business than for any other, and that he should be very much obliged to him all his life for his kindness. "Since this profession is agreeable to you," said the African magician, "I will take you with me to-morrow, and clothe you as richly and handsomely as the best merchants in the city, and after that we will think of opening such a shop as I mean."

Aladdin's mother, who never till then could believe that the magician was her husband's brother, no longer doubted it after his promises of kindness to her son. She thanked him for his good intentions; and after having exhorted Aladdin to render him worthy of his uncle's favour by his good behaviour, served up supper, at which they talked of several indifferent matters; and then the magician, who saw that the night was pretty far advanced, took his leave of the mother and son, and retired.

He came again the next day, as he promised, and took Aladdin with him to a great merchant, who sold all sorts of clothes for different ages and ranks, ready made, and a variety of fine stuffs. He asked to see some that suited Aladdin in size; and after choosing a

9

suit which he liked best, and rejecting others which he did not think handsome enough, he bid Aladdin choose those he preferred. Aladdin, charmed with the liberality of his new uncle, made choice of one, and the magician immediately bought it, and all things necessary, and paid for it without haggling.

When Aladdin found himself so handsomely equipped from top to toe, he returned his uncle all imaginable thanks: who, on the other hand, promised never to forsake him, but always to take him with him; which he did to the most frequented places in the city, and particularly to where the chief merchants kept their shops. When he brought him into the street where they sold the richest stuffs and finest linens, he said to Aladdin, "As you are soon to be a merchant as well as these, it is proper you should frequent these shops, and be acquainted with them." Then he showed him the largest and finest mosques, and took him to the khans or inns where the merchants and travellers lodged, and afterwards to the sultan's palace, where he had free access; and at last he took him to his own khan, where, meeting with some merchants he had got acquainted with since his arrival, he treated them, to make them and his pretended nephew acquainted.

This treat lasted till night, when Aladdin would have taken his leave of his uncle to go home; but the magician would not let him go by himself, but conducted him safe to his mother, who, as soon as she saw him so finely dressed, was transported with joy, and bestowed a thousand blessings upon the magician, for being at so great an expense for her child. "Generous relation!" said she, "I know not how to thank you for your liberality!

10

I know that my son is not deserving of your favours; and was he never so grateful, he would be unworthy of them. For my part," added she, "I thank you with all my soul, and hope you may live long enough to be a witness of my son's gratitude, which he cannot better show than by regulating his conduct by your good advice."

"Aladdin," replied the magician, "is a good boy, and minds well enough, and I believe we shall do very well; but I am sorry for one thing, which is, that I cannot perform to-morrow what I promised, because it is Friday, and the shops will be shut up, and therefore we cannot hire or furnish one, but must leave it till Saturday. But I will call on him to-morrow, and take him to walk in the gardens, where the most fashionable people generally walk. Perhaps he has never seen these amusements, he has only been hitherto among children; but now he must see men." Then the African magician took his leave of the mother and son, and retired. Aladdin, who was overjoyed to be so well clothed, looked forward to the pleasure of walking in the gardens which lay about the town. He had never been out of the town, nor seen the environs, which were very beautiful and pleasant.

Aladdin rose early the next morning, and dressed himself, to be ready when his uncle called on him; and after he had waited some time, he began to be impatient, and stood watching for him at the door; but as soon as he perceived him coming, he told his mother, took leave of her, and ran to meet him.

The magician caressed Aladdin when he came to him. "Come along, my dear child," said he, "and I will show you fine things." Then he led him out at one of the gates of the city, to some large fine houses, or rather palaces, with beautiful gardens, into which anybody might go. At every house he came to, he asked Aladdin if he did not think it fine; and Aladdin was ready to answer, "Here is a finer house, uncle, than any we have seen yet." By this artifice, the cunning magician got Aladdin a good long way into the country; and, pretending to be tired, the better to rest Aladdin, he took the opportunity to sit down in one of the gardens by a fountain of clear water, which fell from a lion's mouth of bronze into a great basin. "Come, nephew," said he, "you must be weary as well as I; let us rest ourselves, and we shall be better able to walk."

After they had sat down, the magician pulled from his girdle a handkerchief with cakes and fruit, which he had provided on purpose, and laid them on the edge of the basin. He broke a cake in two, gave one half to Aladdin, and ate the other himself. During this short repast, he exhorted his nephew to leave off keeping company with children, and to seek that of wise and prudent men, to improve by their conversation; "for," said he, "you will soon be at man's estate, and you cannot too early begin to imitate them." When they had eaten as much as they liked, they got up, and pursued their walk through the gardens, which were separated from one another only by small ditches, which marked out the limits without interrupting the communication: so great was the confidence the inhabitants reposed in each other. By this means, the African magician drew Aladdin insensibly beyond the gardens, and crossed the country, till they almost came to the mountains.

Aladdin, who had never been so far in his life before, began to feel much tired with so long a walk, and said to the magician, "Where are we going, uncle? We have left the gardens a great way behind us, and I see nothing but mountains; if we go much further, I do not know whether I shall be able to reach the town again."

"Never fear, nephew," said the false uncle; "I will show you another garden which surpasses all we have yet seen; it is not far off, it is but a little step; and when we come there, you will say that you would have been sorry to be so near it, and not to have seen it." Aladdin was soon persuaded; and the magician, to make the way seem shorter and less fatiguing, told him a great many stories.

At last they came between two mountains of moderate height and equal size, divided by a narrow valley, which was the place where the magician intended to bring Aladdin, to put into execution a design that had brought him from Africa to China. "We will go no further, now," said he to Aladdin: "I will show you here some very extraordinary things, such as nobody ever saw before; when you have seen them, you will thank me; but while I strike fire, do you gather up all the loose dry sticks you can see, to kindle a fire with."

Aladdin found there so many dried sticks that, before the magician had lighted a match, he had gathered up a great heap. The magician presently set them on fire, and when they were all in a blaze, the magician threw in some incense he had about him, which raised a great cloud of smoke. This he dispersed on each side, by pronouncing several magical words which Aladdin did not understand.

At the same time the earth trembled a little, and opened just before the magician and Aladdin, and showed a stone about half a yard square, laid horizontally, with a brass ring fixed into the middle of it, to raise it up by. Aladdin was so frightened at what he saw, that he would have run away; but he was to be useful to the magician, who caught hold of him, scolded him, and gave him such a box on the ear that he knocked him down, and nearly beat his teeth down his throat. Poor Aladdin got up again trembling, and, with tears in his eyes, said to the magician, "What have I done, uncle, to be treated in this severe manner?"

"I have my reasons for it," replied the magician: "I am your uncle, and supply the place of your father, and you ought to make no reply. But, child," added he, softening, "do not be afraid of anything; for I shall not ask anything of you, except that you should obey me punctually, if you would reap the advantages which I intended you should." These fair promises calmed Aladdin's fears and resentment; and when the magician saw that he was come to himself, he said to him: "You see what I have done by virtue of my incense, and the words I pronounced. Know, then, that under this stone there is hidden a treasure, which is destined to be yours, and which will make you richer than the greatest monarch in the world: this is so true, that no other person but yourself is permitted to touch this stone, and to pull it up and go in; for I am forbidden ever to touch it, or to set foot in this treasure when it is opened; so you must without fail execute what I tell you, for it is a matter of great consequence both to you and to me."

Aladdin, amazed at all he saw and heard the magician say of the treasure, which was to make him happy for ever, forgot what was past, and rising up, said to the magician: "Well, uncle, what is to be done? Command me; I am ready to obey you."

"I am overjoyed, child," said the African magician, embracing him, "to see you make the resolution: come, take hold of the ring, and lift up that stone."

"Indeed, uncle," replied Aladdin, "I am not strong enough to lift it; you must help me."

"You have no occasion for my assistance," answered the magician; "if I help you, we shall not be able to do anything; you must lift it up yourself; take hold of the ring, only pronounce the names of your father and grandfather, then lift it up, and you will find it will come easily." Aladdin did as the magician bade him, and raised the stone with a great deal of ease, and laid it on one side.

When the stone was pulled up, there appeared a cavity about three or four feet deep, with a little door, and steps to go down lower.

"Observe, my son," said the African magician, "what I am going to say to you: go down into that cave, and when you are at the bottom of those steps you will find a door open, which will lead you into a large vaulted place, divided into three great halls, in each of which you will see four large brass vessels placed on each side, full of gold and silver; but take care you do not meddle with them. Before you go into the first hall, be sure to tuck up your gown, and wrap it well about you, and then go through the second into the third without stopping. Above all take care that you do not touch the walls, so much as with your clothes; for if you do, you will die instantly. At the end of the third hall, you will find a door which leads to a garden planted with fine trees loaded with fruit; walk direct across the garden by a path which will lead you to five steps that will bring you upon a terrace, where you will see a niche before you, and in that niche a lighted lamp. Take the lamp down, and put it out; when you have thrown away the wick, and poured out the liquor, put it in your breast and bring it to me. Do not be afraid that the liquor will spoil your clothes, for it is not oil; and the lamp will be dry as soon as it is thrown out. If you have a mind for any of the fruit in the garden, you may gather as much as you please."

After these words, the magician drew a ring off his finger, and put it upon one of Aladdin's, telling him that it was a charm against all evil, so long as he observed what he had prescribed to him. After these instructions he said, "Go down boldly, child, and we shall both be rich all our lives."

Aladdin jumped into the cave, went down the steps, and found the three halls just as the African magician had described them. He went through them with all the precaution the fear of death could inspire; crossed the garden without stopping, took down the lamp from the niche, threw out the wick and the liquor, and, as the magician told him, put it in his bosom. But as he came down from the terrace, he stopped in the garden to observe the fruit, which he had only had a glimpse of in crossing it. All the trees were loaded with extraordinary fruit, of different colours on each tree. Some bore fruit entirely white, and some clear and transparent as crystal; some pale red, and others deeper; some green, blue, and purple, and others yellow: in short there were fruits of all colours. The white were pearls; the clear and transparent, diamonds; the deep red, rubies; the paler, ballas rubies; the green, emeralds; the blue, turquoises; the purple, amethysts; and those that were of yellow cast, sapphires; and so on with the rest. All these fruits were so large and beautiful that nothing was ever seen like them. Aladdin was altogether ignorant of their value, and would have preferred figs and grapes, or any other fruits instead. And though he took them only for coloured glass of little value, yet he was so pleased with the colours and the beauty and extraordinary size of the fruit, that he gathered some of every sort; and accordingly filled his two pockets, and the two new purses his uncle had bought for him with the clothes; and as he could not put them in his pockets, he fastened them to his girdle. Some he wrapped up in the skirts of his gown, which was of silk, large and wrapping, and crammed his breast as full as it could hold.

Having thus loaded himself with riches he knew not the value of, Aladdin returned through the three halls with the same precaution, and made all the haste he could, that he might not make his uncle wait, and soon arrived at the mouth of the cave, where the African magician awaited him with the utmost impatience. As soon as Aladdin saw him, he cried out, "Pray, uncle, lend me your hand, to help me out."

"Give me the lamp first," replied the magician, "it will be troublesome to you."

"Indeed, uncle," answered Aladdin, "I cannot now; it is not troublesome to me: but I will as soon as I am up."

The African magician was so obstinate, that he would have the lamp before he would help him up; and Aladdin, who had encumbered himself so much with his fruit that he could not well get at it, refused to give it to him till he was out of the cave. The African magician, provoked at this obstinate refusal of the lad, flew into a terrible passion, and threw a little of his incense into the fire, which he had taken care to keep in, and no sooner had he pronounced two magical words than the stone which had closed the mouth of the cave moved into its place, with the earth over it, in the same manner as it had been at the arrival of the magician and Aladdin.

This action of the African magician plainly showed him to be neither Aladdin's uncle, nor Mustapha the tailor's brother; but a true African. For as Africa is a country whose inhabitants delight more in magic than those of any other part of the whole world, he had applied himself to it from his youth; and after about forty years' experience in enchantments, fumigations, and reading of magic books, he had found out that there was in the world a wonderful lamp, the possession of which, if he could obtain it, would render him more powerful than any monarch in the world; and by a recent operation he found out that this lamp lay concealed in a subterranean place in the midst of China. Fully persuaded of the truth of this discovery, he set out from the furthest part of Africa; and after a long and fatiguing journey, he came to the town nearest to this treasure. But though he had a certain knowledge of the place where the lamp was, he was not permitted to take it himself, nor to enter the subterranean place where it was, but must receive it from the hands of another person. For

18

this reason he addressed himself to Aladdin, whom he looked upon as a young lad of no consequence, and fit to serve his purpose, resolving, as soon as he got the lamp into his hands, to sacrifice poor Aladdin to his avarice and wickedness by making the fumigation mentioned before, and saying those two magical words, the effect of which was to remove the stone into its place again, that he might have no witness of what he had done.

The blow he gave Aladdin, and the authority he assumed over him, were only to accustom him to fear him, and to make him obey the more readily, and give him the lamp as soon as he asked for it. But his too great hurry in executing his wicked intention on poor Aladdin, and his fear lest somebody should come that way during their dispute and discover what he wished to keep secret, produced an effect quite contrary to what he proposed.

When the African magician saw that all his great hopes were frustrated for ever, he started that same day for Africa; but went quite round the town, and at some distance from it, for fear lest any persons who had seen him walk out with the boy should see him come back without him, entertain suspicions, and stop him.

According to all appearances there was no prospect of Aladdin being heard of any more. But when the magician plotted his death, he had forgotten the ring he put on his finger, which preserved him, though he knew not its virtue; and it is amazing that the loss of that, together with the lamp, did not drive the magician to despair; but magicians are so much used to misfortunes that they do not lay them to heart, but still feed themselves, all their lives, with unsubstantial notions.

As for Aladdin, who never suspected this bad usage from his pretended uncle, after all his caresses and what he had done for him, his surprise is more easily imagined than described. When he found himself buried alive, he cried, and called out to his uncle, to tell him he was ready to give him the lamp; but all in vain, since his cries could not be heard, and he remained in this dark abode. At last, when he had quite tired himself out with crying, he went to the bottom of the steps, to get into the garden, where it was light; but the door, which was opened before by enchantment, was now shut by the same means. Then he redoubled his cries and tears, and sat down on the steps, without any hope of ever seeing the light again, and in a melancholy certainty of passing from the present darkness into a speedy death.

Aladdin remained in this state for two days, without eating or drinking, and on the third day looked upon death as inevitable. Clasping his hands with entire resignation, he said, "There is no strength or power but in the great and high God." In joining his hands he rubbed the ring which the magician had put on his finger, and of which he knew not yet the virtue, and immediately a genie of enormous size and frightful look rose out of the earth, his head reaching the vault, and said to him, "What wouldst thou? I am ready to obey thee as thy slave, and the slave of all who have the ring on thy finger; I and the other slaves of that ring."

At another time, Aladdin, who had not been used to such visions, would have been so frightened, that he would not have been able to speak; but the danger he was in made him answer without hesitation, "Whoever thou art, deliver me from this place, if thou art able."

He had no sooner made an end of these words, than the earth opened, and he found himself on the very spot where the magician had first brought him.

It was some time before Aladdin's eyes could bear the light, after having been so long in total darkness: but after he had endeavoured by degrees to look about him, he was very much surprised not to find the earth open, and could not comprehend how he had got so soon out of it. There was nothing to be seen but the place where the fire had been, by which he could nearly judge whereabouts the cave was. Then turning towards the town, he perceived it in the midst of the gardens that surrounded it, and knew the way back by which the magician had brought him; then, returning God thanks to see himself once more in the world, where he had never expected to be, he made the best of his way home. When he got to his mother's door, his joy at seeing her, and his faintness for want of food for three days, made him swoon, and he remained for a long time as dead. His mother, who had given him over for lost or dead, seeing him in this condition, omitted nothing to bring him to himself again. As soon as he recovered, the first words he spake, were, "Pray, mother, give me something to eat, for I have not put a morsel of anything into my mouth these three days." His mother brought what she had, and set it before him. "My son," said she, "be not too eager, for it is dangerous; eat but a little at a time, and take care of yourself. Besides, I would not have you talk; you will have time enough to tell me what has happened to you, when you have recovered. It is a great comfort to me to see you again, after the grief I have been in since Friday, and the pains

I have taken to learn what had become of you, ever since night came, and you had not returned."

Aladdin took his mother's advice, and ate and drank moderately. When he had done, "Mother," said he, "you believed he was my uncle, as well as I; and what other thoughts could we entertain of a man who was so kind to me? But I must tell you, mother, he is a rogue and a cheat, and only did what he did, and made me all those promises, to accomplish my death; but for what reason neither you nor I can guess. For my part, I can assure you I never gave him any cause to deserve the least ill treatment from him. You shall judge of it yourself, when you have heard all that passed from the time I left you, till he came to the execution of his wicked plan."

Then Aladdin began to tell his mother all that had happened to him from the Friday, when the magician took him to see the palaces and gardens about the town, and what happened on the way, till they came to the place between the two mountains, where the strange deeds were performed; how, with incense which the magician threw into the fire, and some magical words which he pronounced, the earth opened, and discovered a cave, which led to an inestimable treasure. He did not forget the blow the magician gave him, and in what manner he softened again, and got him by great promises, putting a ring on his finger, to go down into the cave. He did not omit the least item of what he saw in crossing the three halls and the garden, and in taking the wonderful lamp, which he showed to his mother, as well as the transparent fruit of different colours, which he had gathered in the garden as he returned. But, though these fruits were precious stones, brilliant as the sun, she was as ignorant of their worth as her son, and cared nothing for them. She had been brought up in a middling rank of life, and her husband's poverty prevented his being possessed of such things, nor had she, or her relations or neighbours, ever seen them; so that we must not wonder that she looked on them as things of no value, and only pleasing to the eye by the variety of their colours.

Aladdin put them behind one of the cushions of the sofa he sat upon, and continued his story. When he came to the end, he said to his mother, "I need say no more; you know the rest. This is my adventure, and the danger I have been exposed to since you saw me."

Aladdin's mother heard, with patience, this surprising and wonderful story, though it caused no small affliction to a mother who loved her son tenderly; but yet in the part which disclosed the perfidy of the African magician, she could not help showing, by the greatest indignation, how much she detested him; and when Aladdin had finished his story, she broke out into a thousand reproaches against that vile impostor. She called him perfidious traitor, barbarian, assassin, deceiver, magician, and an enemy and destroyer of mankind. "Without doubt, child," added she, "he is a magician, and they are plagues to the world, and by their enchantments and sorceries have commerce with the Evil One. Bless God for preserving you from his wicked designs; for your death would have been inevitable, if you had not called upon Him, and implored His assistance." She said a great deal more against the magician's treachery; but finding that whilst she talked her son Aladdin began to nod, she put him to bed.

Aladdin, who had not had one wink of sleep while he was in the subterranean abode, slept very heartily all that night, and never waked till late the next morning; when the first thing he said to his mother was, he wanted something to eat. "Alas! child," said she, "I have not a bit of bread to give you; you ate up all the provisions I had in the house yesterday; but have a little patience, and it shall not be long before I will bring you some: I have a little cotton, which I have spun; I will go and sell it, and buy bread, and something for our dinner."

"Mother," replied Aladdin, "keep your cotton for another time, and give me the lamp I brought home with me yesterday; I will go and sell that, and the money I shall get for it will serve both for breakfast and dinner, and perhaps supper too."

Aladdin's mother took the lamp, and said to her son, "Here it is, but it is very dirty; if it was a little cleaner I believe it would fetch something more." She took a little fine sand and water to clean it; but no sooner had she begun to rub it than a hideous genie of gigantic size appeared before her, and said in a voice like thunder, "What wouldst thou have? I am ready to obey thee as thy slave, and the slave of all those who have that lamp in their hands; I, and the other slaves of the lamp."

Aladdin's mother was not able to speak at the sight of this frightful genie, but fainted away; when Aladdin, who had seen such a genie in the cavern, without losing time on reflection, snatched the lamp out of his mother's hands, and said to the genie boldly, "I am hungry; bring me something to eat." The genie disappeared immediately, and in an instant returned with a large silver basin on his head, and twelve covered plates of the same metal, which contained excellent meats; six large white loaves on two other plates, two bottles of wine, and two silver cups in his hands. All these things he placed upon a table, and disappeared; and all this was done before Aladdin's mother came out of her swoon.

Aladdin went and fetched some water, and threw it on her face, to recover her. Whether that or the smell of the meats the genie procured brought her to life again, it was not long before she came to herself. "Mother," said Aladdin, "do not mind this; it is nothing at all; get up, and come and eat; do not let such fine meat get cold, but fall to."

His mother was very much surprised to see the great basin, twelve plates, six loaves, and the two bottles and cups, and to smell the delicious odour which exhaled from the plates. "Child," said she to Aladdin, "to whom are we indebted for this great plenty? Has the sultan been made acquainted with our poverty, and had compassion on us?"

"It is no matter, mother," said Aladdin; "let us sit down and eat; for you are in almost as much need of a good breakfast as myself; when we have done, I will tell you." Accordingly both mother and son sat down, and ate with first-rate appetites. But all the time Aladdin's mother could not forbear looking at and admiring the basin and plates, though she could not well tell whether they were silver or any other metal, so little accustomed were she and her son to see such things.

In short, the mother and son sat at breakfast till it was dinner-time, and then they thought it would be best to put the two meals together; yet after this they found they should have enough left for supper, and two meals for the next day.

When Aladdin's mother had taken away and set by what was left, she went and sat down by her son on the sofa. "Aladdin," said she, "I expect now that you should tell me exactly what passed between the genie and you while I was in a swoon;" which he at once complied with.

She was in as great amazement at what her son told her as at the appearance of the genie; and said to him, "But, son, what have we to do with genies? I never in my life heard that any of my acquaintance had ever seen one. How came that vile genie to address himself to me, and not to you, to whom he had appeared before in the cave?"

"Mother," answered Aladdin, "the genie you saw is not the same who appeared to me, though he resembles him in size; no, they had quite a different appearance and habits; they belong to different masters. If you remember, he that I first saw called himself the slave of the ring on my finger; and this one you saw called himself the slave of the lamp you had in your hand: but you did not hear him, for I think you fainted away as soon he began to speak."

"What!" cried his mother, "was your lamp the occasion of that cursed genie's addressing himself to me rather than to you. Ah! my son, take it out of my sight, and put it where you please. I will never touch it. I had rather you would sell it than run the risk of being frightened to death again by touching it: and if you would take my advice, you would part also with the ring, and not have anything to do with genies, who, as our prophet has told us, are only devils."

"With your leave, mother," replied Aladdin, "I shall take care how I sell a lamp which may be so serviceable both to you and me. Have you not seen what it has procured us? It shall still continue to furnish us with subsistence. My false and wicked uncle would not have taken so much pains, and undertaken so long and tedious a journey, if it had not been to get into his possession this wonderful lamp, which he preferred before all the gold and silver which he knew was in the halls, and which I have seen with my own eyes. He knew too well the merit and worth of this lamp; and since chance has shown the virtue of it to us, let us make a profitable use of it, without making any great stir, and drawing the envy and jealousy of our neighbours upon us. However, since the genies frighten you so much, I will take it out of your sight, and put it where I may find it when I want it. As for the ring, I cannot resolve to part with that either, for without that you would never have seen me again; and though I am alive now, perhaps, if it was gone, I might not be so some moments hence; therefore I hope you will give me leave to keep that, and to wear it always on my finger. Who knows what dangers you and I may be exposed to, which neither of us can foresee, and from which it may deliver us?"

As Aladdin's arguments were just, and had great weight, his mother had nothing to say against them; but only replied, that he might do what he pleased, but for her part she would have nothing to do with genies, but would wash her hands of them, and never say anything more about them.

By the next day they had eaten all the provisions the genie had brought; and the next day Aladdin, who could not bear the thought of hunger, took one of the silver plates under his coat and went out early to sell it, and addressing himself to a merchant whom he met in the streets, took him aside, and pulling out the plate, asked him if he would buy it. The cunning merchant took the plate and examined it, and no sooner found that it was good silver than he asked Aladdin at how much he valued it. Aladdin, who knew not the value of it, and never had been used to such traffic, told him he would trust to his judgment and honour. The merchant was somewhat taken aback at this plain dealing; and, doubting whether Aladdin understood the material or the full value of what he offered him, he took a piece of gold out of his purse and gave it him, though it was but the sixtieth part of the worth of the plate. Aladdin took the money very eagerly, and as soon as he got it in his pocket, retired with so much haste, that the merchant, not content with his exorbitant profit, was vexed he had not penetrated into Aladdin's ignorance, and was going to run after him to get some change out of the piece of gold; but Aladdin ran so fast, and had got so far, that it would have been impossible to overtake him.

Before Aladdin went home to his mother, he called at a baker's, bought a loaf, changed his money, and went home, and gave the rest to his mother, who went and bought provisions enough to last them some time. After this manner they lived, till Aladdin had sold the twelve plates, one at a time, to the merchant, for the same money; who, after the first time, durst not offer him less, for fear of losing so good a customer. When he had sold the last plate, he had recourse to the basin, which weighed ten times as much as the plate and would have carried it to his old purchaser, except that it was too large and cumbersome; therefore he was obliged to bring him home with him to his mother's, where, after the merchant had examined the weight of the basin, he laid down ten pieces of gold, with which Aladdin was very well satisfied.

They lived on these ten pieces in a frugal manner a good while; and Aladdin, though formerly used to an idle life, had left off playing with young lads of his own age ever since his adventure with the African magician. He spent his time in walking about, and talking with people with whom he had got acquainted. Sometimes he would stop at the best merchants' shops, where people of distinction met, and listen to their talk, by which he gained some little knowledge of the world.

When all the money was spent, Aladdin had recourse again to the lamp. He took it in his hand, looked for the place where his mother had rubbed it with the sand, and rubbed it also, and the genie immediately appeared, and said, "What wouldst thou have? I am ready to obey thee as thy slave and the slave of those who have that lamp in their hands; I, and the other slaves of the lamp."

"I am hungry," said Aladdin; "bring me something to eat."

The genie disappeared, and presently returned with a basin, and the same number of covered plates, etc., and set them down on a table, and vanished again.

Aladdin's mother, knowing what her son was going to do, went out at that time about some business, on purpose to avoid being in the way when the genie came;

29

and when she returned, which was not long afterwards, and found the table and sideboard so furnished a second time, she was almost as much surprised as before at the prodigious effect of the lamp. However she sat down with her son, and when they had eaten as much as they wanted, she set enough by to last them two or three days.

As soon as Aladdin found that their provisions and money were spent, he took one of these plates, and went to look for the merchant again; but as he passed by the shop of a goldsmith, who had the character of a very fair and honest man, the goldsmith called to him, and said, "My lad, I have often observed you go by, loaded as you are at present, and talk with a certain merchant, and then come back again empty-handed. I imagine that you carry something to sell to him; but perhaps you do not know what a rogue he is; he is the greatest rogue among all the merchants, and is so well known that nobody will have anything to do with him. What I tell you is for your own good. If you will show me what you now carry, and if it is to be sold, I will give you the full value of it; or I will direct you to other merchants who will not cheat you."

The hope of getting more money for this plate induced Aladdin to pull it from under his coat and show it to the goldsmith. The old man, who at first sight saw that it was made of the finest silver, asked him if he had sold any such as that to the merchant, and Aladdin told him plainly that he had sold him twelve such for a piece of gold each.

"What a villain!" cried the goldsmith; "but," added he, "my son, what is past cannot be recalled. By showing you the value of this plate, which is of the finest silver we use in our shops, I will let you see how much the merchant has cheated you."

The goldsmith took a pair of scales, weighed the plate, and after he had told Aladdin how much an ounce of fine silver was worth, he showed him that his plate was worth by weight sixty pieces of gold, which he paid him down immediately. "If you dispute my honesty," said he, "you may go to any other of our trade, and if he gives you any more, I will forfeit twice as much."

Aladdin thanked him for his good advice, so greatly to his advantage, and never after went to any other person, but sold him all his plates and the basin, and had as much for them as the weight came to.

Though Aladdin and this mother had an inexhaustible treasure of money in their lamp, and might have had whatever they had a mind to, yet they lived with the same frugality as before, except that Aladdin went more neat; as for his mother, she wore no clothes but what she earned by spinning cotton. Hence the money for which Aladdin had sold the plates and basin was sufficient to maintain them some time. They went on for many years by the help of the produce that Aladdin, from time to time, made of his lamp.

During this time Aladdin frequented the shops of the principal merchants, where they sold cloth of gold and silver, and linens, silk stuffs and jewellery, and oftentimes joining in their conversation, acquired a complete knowledge of the world, and assumed its manners. From his acquaintance with the jewellers, he came to know that the fine fruit which he had gathered, when he took the lamp, was not coloured glass, but stones of extraordinary value. For as he had seen all sorts of jewels bought and sold in the shops, but none so beautiful or so large as his, he found that instead of coloured glass he possessed an inestimable treasure; but he had the prudence not to say anything of it to any one.

One day, as Aladdin was walking about the town, he chanced to see the Princess Badroulboudour, the sultan's daughter, attended by a great crowd of ladies, slaves, and attendants, just at a moment when she unveiled her face. Aladdin had never seen any woman unveiled except his mother, and the princess was so beautiful that he was filled with amazement, and could think of nothing else for several days and nights. At last his mother inquired why he was so silent and absent-minded. "Mother," said Aladdin, "I cannot live without the beautiful and amiable Princess Badroulboudour, and I am firmly resolved to ask her in marriage from her father."

Aladdin's mother listened with attention to what her son told her; but when he talked of asking the Princess Badroulboudour in marriage of the sultan, she could not help bursting out into a loud laugh. Aladdin would have gone on, but she interrupted him: "Alas! child," said she, "what are you thinking of? you must be mad to talk so."

"I assure you, mother," replied Aladdin, "that I am not mad, but in my right senses: I foresaw that you would reproach me for folly and extravagance; but I must tell you once more, that I am resolved to demand the Princess Badroulboudour of the sultan in marriage, and your remonstrances shall not prevent me."

"Indeed, son," replied his mother, seriously, "I cannot help telling you that you have quite forgotten yourself; and I do not see who you can get to venture to propose it for you."

"You, yourself," replied he immediately.

"I go to the sultan!" answered his mother, amazed and surprised. "I shall take good care how I engage in such an affair. Why, who are you, son," continued she, "that you can have the assurance to think of your sultan's daughter? Have you forgotten that your father was one of the poorest tailors in the capital, and that I am of no better extraction; and do not you know that sultans never marry their daughters but to princes, sons of sultans like themselves?"

"Mother," answered Aladdin, "I have already told you that I foresaw all that you have said, or can say: and tell you again that neither your discourse nor your remonstrances shall make me change my mind. I have told you that you must ask the Princess Badroulboudour in marriage for me: it is a favour I request with all the respect I owe you; and I beg of you not to refuse me, unless you would rather see me in my grave, than by so doing give me new life."

The good old woman was very much embarrassed, when she found Aladdin so obstinately persisting in so foolish a design. "My son," said she again, "I am your mother, and there is nothing reasonable that I would not readily do for you. If I were to go and treat about your marriage with some neighbour's daughter, whose circumstances were equal to yours, I would do it with all my heart; and even then they would expect you to have some little estate or fortune, or

be of some trade. When such poor folks as we are to
marry, the first thing they ought to think of is how to
live. But without reflecting on your lowly birth, and the
little merit and fortune you have to recommend you,
you aim at the highest; you demand in marriage the
daughter of your sovereign, who with one single word
can crush you to pieces. How could so extraordinary
a thought come into your head, as that I should go
to the sultan, and make a proposal to him to give his
daughter in marriage to you? Suppose I had, not to
say the boldness, but the impudence to present myself
before the sultan and make so extravagant a request, to
whom should I address myself to be introduced to his
majesty? Do you not think the first person I should speak
to would take me for a mad woman, and chastise me as I
should deserve? Of course, I know there is no difficulty
to those who go to ask justice, which he distributes
equally among his subjects; I know too that to those
who ask some favour he grants it with pleasure when
he sees that it is deserved, and the persons are worthy
of it. But is that your case? And do you think you have
deserved the favour you would have me ask for you?
Are you worthy of it? What have you done, either for
your prince or country? How have you distinguished
yourself? If you have done nothing to merit so great a
favour, nor are worthy of it, with what face shall I ask
it? How can I open my mouth to make such a proposal
to the sultan? His majestic presence and the splendour
of his court would immediately silence me. There is
another reason, my son, which you do not think of;
nobody ever goes to ask a favour of the sultan without
a present. But what presents have you to make? And

if you had any that was worthy of the least attention of so great a monarch, what proportion could it bear to the favour you would ask? Therefore, reflect well on what you are about, and consider that you aspire to a thing which it is impossible for you to obtain."

Aladdin heard very calmly all that his mother could say to dissuade him from his design, and made answer: "I own, mother, it is great rashness in me to presume so far; and a great want of consideration to ask you with so much suddenness to go and make the proposal of my marriage to the sultan, without first taking proper measures to procure a favourable reception; I therefore beg your pardon. But be not surprised that I did not at first sight see everything that it was necessary to do to procure me the happiness I seek after. I love the Princess Badroulboudour beyond everything you can imagine; and shall always persevere in my design of marrying her, which is a thing I have determined and resolved on. I am much obliged to you for the hint you have given me, and look upon it as the first step I ought to take.

"You say it is not customary to go to the sultan without a present, and that I have nothing worthy of his acceptance. As to what you say about the present, do you not think, mother, that what I brought home with me the day on which I was delivered from certain death, may be an agreeable present? I mean those things you and I both took for coloured glass; they are jewels of inestimable value, and fit for the greatest monarch. I know the worth of them through frequenting the jewellers' shops; and you may take my word for it, all the jewels that I have seen in the best jewellers' shops were not to be compared to those we have, either for size or beauty. Neither you nor I know the value of ours; but I am persuaded that they will be received very favourably by the sultan; you have a large porcelain dish fit to hold them; fetch it, and let us see how they will look, when we have arranged them according to their different colours."

Aladdin's mother fetched the china dish, and he took the jewels out of the two purses in which he had kept them, and placed them in the dish. But the brightness and lustre they had in the daytime, and the variety of the colours, so dazzled the eyes of both mother and son that they were astonished beyond measure; for they had only seen them by the light of a lamp; and though Aladdin had seen them hang on the trees like fruit, beautiful to the eye, yet as he was then but a boy, he did not take much notice of them.

After they had admired the beauty of this present some time, Aladdin said to his mother, "Now you cannot excuse yourself from going to the sultan, under the pretext of not having a present to make him, since here is one which will gain you a favourable reception."

Though Aladdin's mother did not believe it to be so valuable as her son esteemed it, she thought it might nevertheless be agreeable to the sultan, and found that she had not anything to say against it, but kept thinking of the request Aladdin wanted her to make to the sultan. "My son," said she, "I cannot conceive that your present will have its desired effect, and that the sultan will message of yours, I shall have no power to open my mouth; and, therefore, I shall not only lose my labour, but the present, which you say is so extraordinarily valuable, and shall return home again in confusion. I have told you the consequences, and you ought to believe me; but," added she, "I will do my best to please you; though certainly he will either laugh at me, or send me back like a fool, or be in so great a rage as to make us both the victims of his fury."

She used a great many more arguments to make him change his mind; but Aladdin persisted, and his mother, as much out of tenderness as for fear he should be guilty of some worse piece of extravagance, consented.

As it was now late, and the time for going to the sultan's palace was past, it was put off till the next day. The mother and son talked of different matters the remaining part of the day; and Aladdin took a great deal of pains to encourage his mother in the task she had undertaken; while she, notwithstanding all his arguments, could not persuade herself that she could ever succeed; and it must be confessed she had reason enough to doubt. "Child," said she to Aladdin, "if the sultan should receive me as favourably as I wish for your sake, and hear my proposal with calmness, and after this kind reception should think of asking me where lie your riches and your estate (for he will sooner enquire after these than your person), if, I say, he should ask me the question, what answer would you have me give him?"

"Let us not be uneasy, mother," replied Aladdin, "about what may never happen. First, let us see how the sultan receives you, and what answer he gives. If it should so happen that he desires to be informed of all that you mention, I have thought of an answer, and am confident that the lamp, which has assisted us so long, will not fail me in time of need."

Aladdin's mother could not say anything against what her son then proposed; but reflected that the lamp might be capable of doing greater wonders than merely providing food for them. This satisfied her, and at the same time removed all the difficulties which might have prevented her from undertaking the service she had promised her son; when Aladdin, who penetrated into his mother's thoughts, said to her, "Above all things, mother, be sure to keep the secret, for thereon depends the success;" and after this caution, Aladdin and his mother parted to go to bed. Aladdin rose at daybreak, and went and awakened his mother, begging her to get dressed to go to the sultan's palace, and to get in first, as the grand vizier, the other viziers, and all the great officers of state went in to take their seats in the divan, where the sultan always presided in person.

Aladdin's mother did all that her son desired. She took the china dish, in which they had put the jewels the day before, tied up in two napkins, one finer than the other, and set out for the sultan's palace, to the great satisfaction of Aladdin. When she came to the gates, the grand vizier, and the other viziers and most distinguished lords of the court, were just gone in; and, notwithstanding the crowd of people who had business there, which was extraordinarily great, she got into the divan, which was a large spacious hall. She placed herself just before the sultan, the grand vizier, and the great lords, who sat in that council, on his right and left hand. Several cases were called, according to their order, and pleaded and adjudged, until the time the divan generally broke up, when the sultan rising, dismissed the council, and returned to his apartment, attended by the grand vizier; the other viziers and ministers of state returned, as also did all those whose business called them thither; some pleased with gaining their cases, others dissatisfied at the sentences pronounced against them, and some in expectation of theirs being heard at the next sitting.

Aladdin's mother, seeing the sultan rise and retire, and all the people go away, rightly judged that he would not come again that day, and resolved to go home. When Aladdin saw her return with the present, he knew not at first what to think, and from the fear he was in lest she should bring him some bad news, he had not courage enough to ask her any questions, till his mother, who had never set foot in the sultan's palace before, and knew not what was done there every day, freed him from his embarrassment, and said, "Son, I have seen the sultan, and am very well persuaded he has seen me too; for I placed myself just before him, and nothing could hinder him from seeing me; but he was so much taken up with all those who talked on all sides of him, that I pitied him, and wondered at his patience to hear them. At last I believe he was heartily tired, for he rose up suddenly, and would not hear a great many who were prepared to speak to him, but went away, at which I was very well pleased, for indeed I began to lose all patience, and was extremely tired with staying so long. But there is no harm done; I will go again to-morrow; perhaps the sultan may not be so busy."

Though Aladdin was very violent, he was forced to be satisfied with this, and to fortify himself with patience. He had at least the satisfaction of finding that

39

his mother had got over the greatest difficulty, which was to procure access to the sultan, and hoped that the example of those whom she saw speak to him would embolden her to acquit herself better when a favourable opportunity offered.

The next morning she went to the sultan's palace with the present, as early as the day before, but when she came there, she found the gates of the divan shut, and understood that the council only sat every other day, and that therefore she must come again the next. This news she carried to her son, whose only relief was patience. She went six times afterwards on the days appointed, placed herself always directly before the sultan, but with as little success as on the first time, and might have perhaps come a thousand times to as little purpose, if the sultan himself had not taken particular notice of her.

At last, after the council had broken up, and when the sultan returned to his own apartment, he said to his grand vizier, "I have for some time observed a certain woman, who comes constantly every day that I go into council, and has something wrapped up in a napkin: she always stands up from the beginning of the breaking up of the council, and places herself just before me. Do you know what she wants?"

"Sir," replied the grand vizier, who knew no more than the sultan, but did not like to seem uninformed, "perhaps this woman has come to complain to your majesty that somebody has sold her some bad flour, or some such trifling matter." The sultan was not satisfied with this answer, but replied, "If this woman comes again next council-day, do not fail to call her, that I may hear what she has to say." The grand vizier made answer by kissing his hand, and lifting it up above his head, signifying his willingness to lose it if he failed.

By this time, Aladdin's mother was so much accustomed to go to the council, and stand before the sultan, that she did not think it any trouble, if she could but satisfy her son that she neglected nothing that lay in her power: so the next council-day she went to the divan, and placed herself before the sultan as usual; and before the grand vizier had made his report of business, the sultan perceived her, and compassionating her for having waited so long, he said to the vizier, "Before you enter upon any business, remember the woman I spoke to you about: bid her come near, and let us hear and despatch her business first." The grand vizier immediately called the chief of the officers; and pointing to her, bade him go to the woman, and tell her to come before the sultan.

The chief of the officers went to Aladdin's mother, and at a sign she followed him to the foot of the sultan's throne, where he left her, and retired to his place by the grand vizier. Aladdin's mother, following the example of a great many others whom she saw salute the sultan, bowed her head down to the carpet, which covered the steps of the throne, and remained in that posture till the sultan bade her rise, which she had no sooner done than the sultan said to her, "Good woman, I have observed you a long time; what business brings you here?"

At these words, Aladdin's mother prostrated herself a second time; and when she got up again, said, "Monarch of monarchs, before I tell your majesty the extraordinary and almost incredible business which brings me before your high throne, I beg of you to pardon the boldness or rather impudence of the demand I am going to make, which is so uncommon that I tremble, and am ashamed to propose it to my sultan." In order to give her the more freedom to explain herself, the sultan ordered everybody to go out of the divan but the grand vizier, and then told her she might speak without restraint.

Aladdin's mother, notwithstanding this favour of the sultan's to save her the trouble and confusion of speaking before so many people, was not a little apprehensive; therefore, she said, "I beg your majesty, if you should think my demand the least injurious or offensive, to assure me first of your pardon and forgiveness."

"Well," replied the sultan, "I will forgive you, be it what it will, and no hurt shall come to you: speak boldly."

When Aladdin's mother had taken all these precautions, for fear of the sultan's anger, she told him faithfully how Aladdin had seen the Princess Badroulboudour, and had fallen in love with her, the declaration he had made to her when he came home, and what she had said to dissuade him, "But," continued she, "my son, instead of taking my advice and reflecting on his boldness, was so obstinate as to threaten me with some desperate act if I refused to come and ask the princess in marriage of your majesty; and it was not till after doing violence to my feelings that I was forced to come, for which I beg your majesty once more to pardon not only me, but Aladdin my son for entertaining such a rash thought."

The sultan hearkened mildly, without showing the least anger; but before he gave her any answer, he asked her what she had brought tied up in that napkin.

She took the china dish, which she had set down at the foot of the throne, before she prostrated herself before him; she untied it, and presented it to the sultan.

The sultan's amazement and surprise were inexpressible, when he saw so many large, beautiful, and valuable jewels collected in one dish. He remained for some time motionless with admiration. At last, when he had recovered himself, he received the present from Aladdin's mother's hand, crying out in a transport of joy, "How rich and how beautiful!" After he had admired and handled all the jewels, one after another, he turned about to his grand vizier, and showing him the dish, said, "Look here, and confess that your eyes never beheld anything so rich and beautiful before." The vizier was charmed. "Well," continued the sultan, "what sayest thou to such a present? Is it not worthy of the princess my daughter? And ought I not to bestow her on one who values her at so great a price?"

These words put the grand vizier into a great fright. The sultan had some time before signified to him his intention of bestowing the princess his daughter on a son of his; therefore he was afraid, and not without grounds, that the sultan might change his mind. Thereupon, going up to him, and whispering he said, "Sir, I cannot but own that the present is worthy of the princess; but I beg of your majesty to grant me three months before you come to a decision. I hope before that time that my son, on whom you have had the goodness to look with a favourable eye, will be able to make a nobler present than Aladdin, who is an entire stranger to your majesty."

Though the sultan was very sure that it was not

possible for the vizier to provide so considerable a present for his son to make, he hearkened to him, and granted the favour. So turning to Aladdin's mother, he said to her, "Good woman, go home, and tell your son that I agree to the proposal you have made me; but I cannot marry the princess my daughter till some furniture I intend for her be got ready, which cannot be finished for three months; but at the end of that time come again."

Aladdin's mother returned home much more overjoyed than she could have imagined, and told Aladdin all that had happened.

Aladdin thought himself the most happy of all men at hearing this news, and thanked his mother for all the pains she had taken. When two of the three months were past, his mother one evening went to light the lamp, and finding no oil in the house, went out to buy some, and when she came into the city, found a general rejoicing. The shops, instead of being shut up, were open. The streets were crowded with officers in robes of ceremony, mounted on horses richly caparisoned, each attended by a great many footmen. Aladdin's mother asked the oil-merchant what was the meaning of all these doings. "Whence come you, good woman," said he, "that you don't know that the grand vizier's son is to marry the Princess Badroulboudour, the sultan's daughter, to-night? These officers that you see are to assist at the procession to the palace, where the ceremony is to be solemnised."

This was news enough for Aladdin's mother. She ran till she was quite out of breath home to her son, who little suspected any such thing. "Child," cried she, "you are undone! you depend upon the sultan's fine promises, but they will come to nothing." Aladdin was terribly alarmed at these words. "Mother," replied he, "how do you know the sultan has been guilty of breaking his promise?"

"This night," answered his mother, "the grand vizier's son is to marry the Princess Badroulboudour." She then related how she had heard it; so that he had no reason to doubt the truth of what she said.

At this Aladdin was thunderstruck. Any other man would have sunk under the shock; but soon he bethought himself of the lamp, which had till then been so useful to him; and without venting his rage in empty words against the sultan, the vizier, or his son, he only said, "Perhaps, mother, the vizier's son may not be so happy to-night as he thinks: while I go into my room, do you go and get supper ready." She accordingly went about it, and guessed that her son was going to make use of the lamp, to prevent the marriage if possible.

When Aladdin had got into his room, he took the lamp, and rubbed it in the same place as before, and immediately the genie appeared, and said to him, "What wouldst thou have? I am ready to obey thee as thy slave, and the slave of all those who have that lamp in their hands; I and the other slaves of the lamp."

"Hear me," said Aladdin; "thou hast hitherto brought me whatever I wanted as to provisions; but now I have business of the greatest importance for thee to execute. I have demanded the Princess Badroulboudour in marriage of the sultan her father; he promised her to me, but only asked three months' time; and instead of keeping that promise, he has planned to marry her to

45

the grand vizier's son. I have just heard this, and have no doubt of it. What I ask of you is, that you bring them both hither to me."

"Master," replied the genie, "I will obey you. Have you any other commands?"

"None at present," answered Aladdin; and then the genie disappeared.

Aladdin went downstairs to his mother, with the same tranquillity of mind as usual; and after supper talked of the princess's marriage as of an affair wherein he had not the least concern; and afterwards sat up till the genie had executed his orders.

In the mean time, everything was prepared with the greatest magnificence in the sultan's palace to celebrate the princess's wedding; and the evening was spent with all the usual ceremonies and great rejoicings.

Suddenly the genie, as the faithful slave of the lamp, to the great amazement of bride and bridegroom, took them up, and transported them in an instant to Aladdin's house, where he set them down.

Aladdin had waited impatiently for this moment. "Take this man," said he to the genie, "and shut him up, and come again tomorrow." The genie took the vizier's son and carried him away; and after he had breathed upon him, which prevented his stirring, he left him.

Great as was Aladdin's love for the Princess Badroulboudour, he did not talk much to her, but only said, "Fear nothing, adorable princess; you are in safety. If I have been forced to come to this extremity, it is not with any intention of affronting you, but to prevent an unjust rival's marrying you contrary to the sultan your father's promise to me."

The princess, who knew nothing of these particulars, gave very little attention to what Aladdin said. The fright and amazement of so surprising and unexpected an adventure had put her into such a condition that he could not get one word from her.

Next morning the genie came at the hour appointed, and said to him, "I am here, master; what are your commands?"

"Go," said Aladdin, "fetch the vizier's son out of the place where you left him, and then take them back to the sultan's palace." The genie presently returned with the vizier's son, and in an instant they were transported into the palace. But we must observe, that all this time the genie never appeared to either the princess or the grand vizier's son. His hideous form would have made them die with fear. Neither did they hear anything of the discourse between Aladdin and him; they only perceived the motion, and their transportation from one place to another; which we may well imagine was enough to frighten them.

Next day the princess was very melancholy and alarmed, and the sultan and his wife thought she must either be mad, or else have had a bad dream.

The rejoicings lasted all that day in the palace, and the sultaness, who never left the princess, did all she could to divert her.

But the princess continued so gloomy and ill-tempered that the sultan, provoked with his daughter, said to her in a rage, with his sabre in his hand, "Daughter, tell me what is the matter, or I will cut off your head immediately."

The princess, more frightened at the menaces and

tone of the enraged sultan than at the sight of the drawn sabre, at last broke silence, and said, with tears in her eyes, "My dear father the sultan, I ask your majesty's pardon if I have offended you, and hope you will have compassion on me when I have told you what a dreadful thing has happened." Then she told him all.

The sultan felt extreme uneasiness at so surprising an adventure. "Daughter," said he, "efface all these troublesome ideas out of your memory; I will take care and give orders that you shall have no more such disagreeable and insupportable adventures."

As soon as the sultan got back to his own apartment, he sent for the grand vizier. "Vizier," said he, "have you seen your son, and has he told you anything?"

The vizier replied, "No."

Then the sultan related all that the Princess Badroulboudour had told him, and said, "I do not doubt that my daughter has told me the truth; but nevertheless I should be glad to have it confirmed by your son; therefore go and ask him."

The grand vizier went immediately to his son, and communicated what the sultan had told him, and enjoined him to conceal nothing, but to tell him the whole truth.

"I will disguise nothing from you, father," replied the son, "for indeed all that the princess says is true. All this ill-usage does not the least lessen the respect and gratitude I entertain for the princess, and of which she is so deserving; but I must confess that, notwithstanding all the honour and splendour that attends my marrying my sovereign's daughter, I would much rather die than marry her if I must undergo again what I have already endured. I do not doubt but that the princess entertains the same sentiments, and that she will readily agree to part, which is so necessary both for her repose and mine. Therefore, father, I beg you to get the sultan's consent that our marriage may be broken off."

Notwithstanding the grand vizier's ambition to have his son allied to the sultan, the firm resolution which he saw he had formed to be separated from the princess made him go and give the sultan an account of what he had told him, assuring him that all was but too true, and begging him to give his son leave to retire from the palace, alleging, for an excuse, that it was not just that the princess should be a moment longer exposed to so terrible a persecution upon his son's account.

The grand vizier found no great difficulty in obtaining what he asked. From that instant the sultan, who had determined upon it already, gave orders to put a stop to all rejoicings in the palace and town, and sent post-haste to all parts of his dominions to countermand his first orders; and in a short time all rejoicings ceased.

This sudden and unexpected change gave rise, in both the city and kingdom, to various speculations and inquiries; but no other account could be given of it except that both the vizier and his son went out of the palace very much dejected. Nobody but Aladdin knew the secret. He rejoiced over the happy success procured for him by his lamp. But neither the sultan nor the grand vizier, who had forgotten Aladdin and his request, had the least thought that he had any hand in the enchantment which caused the marriage to be broken off.

Nevertheless, Aladdin waited till the three months

were completed, which the sultan had appointed for the marriage between the Princess Badroulboudour and himself; but the next day sent his mother to the palace, to remind the sultan of his promise.

Aladdin's mother went to the palace, as her son had bidden her, and stood before the divan in the same place as before. The sultan no sooner cast his eyes upon her than he knew her again, and remembered her business, and how long he had put her off: therefore when the grand vizier was beginning to make his report, the sultan interrupted him, and said, "Vizier, I see the good woman who made me the present some months ago; forbear your report till I have heard what she has to say." The vizier presently perceived Aladdin's mother, and sent the chief of the officers for her.

Aladdin's mother came to the foot of the throne, and prostrated herself as usual, and when she rose up again, the sultan asked her what she wanted. "Sir," said she, "I come to represent to your majesty, in the name of my son Aladdin, that the three months, at the end of which you ordered me to come again, are expired; and to beg you to remember your promise."

The sultan had little thought of hearing any more of a marriage which he imagined would be very disagreeable to the princess, when he considered only the meanness and poverty of Aladdin's mother, and this summons for him to be as good as his word was somewhat embarrassing to him; he declined giving an answer till he had consulted his vizier.

The grand vizier freely told the sultan his thoughts on the matter, and said to him, "In my opinion, sir, there is one certain way for your majesty to avoid so unequal a match without giving Aladdin any cause of complaint; which is, to set so high a value upon the princess, that were he never so rich, he could not come up to it. This is the only way to make him desist from so bold, not to say rash, an undertaking."

The sultan, approving of the grand vizier's advice, turned about to Aladdin's mother, and after some reflection, said to her, "Good woman, it is true sultans ought to be as good as their word, and I am ready to keep mine, by making your son happy by his marriage with the princess my daughter. But as I cannot marry her without some valuable present from your son, you may tell him, I will fulfil my promise as soon as he shall send me forty basins of massy gold, brim-full of the same things you have already made me a present of, and carried by the like number of black slaves, who shall be led by as many young and handsome white slaves, all dressed magnificently. On these conditions I am ready to bestow the princess my daughter on him; therefore, good woman, go and tell him so, and I will wait till you bring me his answer."

Aladdin's mother prostrated herself a second time before the sultan's throne, and retired. On her way home she laughed to herself at her son's foolish imagination. "Where," said she, "can he get so many large gold basins, and enough of that coloured glass to fill them? Must he go again to that subterranean abode, the entrance into which is stopped up, and gather them off the trees? But where will he get so many slaves such as the sultan requires? It is altogether out of his power, and I believe he will not be so well satisfied with my embassy this time." When she came home, full of these thoughts, she said to her son, "Indeed, child, I would not have you think any further of your marriage with the Princess Badroulboudour. The sultan received me very kindly, and I believe he was well disposed to you; but if I am not very much deceived, the grand vizier has made him change his mind." Then she gave her son an exact account of what the sultan said to her, and the conditions on which he consented to the match. Afterwards she said to him, "The sultan expects your answer immediately; but," continued she, laughing, "I believe he may wait long enough."

"Not so long, mother, as you imagine," replied Aladdin; "the sultan is mistaken if he thinks by this exorbitant demand to prevent my entertaining thoughts of the princess; his demand is but a trifle to what I could have done for her. But go and get us something for dinner, and leave the rest to me."

As soon as Aladdin's mother was gone out to the market, Aladdin took the lamp, and rubbed it; the genie appeared, and offered his services as usual. "The sultan," said Aladdin to him, "demands forty large basins of massy gold, brim-full of the fruits of the garden from whence I took this lamp you are slave to; and these he expects to have carried by as many black slaves, each preceded by a young, handsome, well-made white slave, richly clothed. Go and fetch me this present as soon as possible, that I may send it to him before the divan breaks up." The genie told him his command should be immediately obeyed, and disappeared.

A little while afterwards the genie returned with forty black slaves, each bearing on his head a basin of massy gold of twenty marks' weight, full of pearls, diamonds, rubies, and emeralds, all larger and more beautiful than those presented to the sultan before. Each basin was covered with a silver stuff, embroidered with flowers of gold: all these, and the white slaves, quite filled the house, which was but a small one, and the little court before it, and a little garden behind. The genie asked Aladdin if he had any other commands. Aladdin told him that he wanted nothing further then, and the genie disappeared.

When Aladdin's mother came back from the market, she was greatly surprised to see so many people and such vast riches. As soon as she had laid down her provisions, Aladdin said, "Mother, let us lose no time; before the sultan and the divan rise, I would have you return to the palace, and go with this present as the dowry he asked for the Princess Badroulboudour, that he may judge by my diligence and exactness how anxious I am to procure the honour of this alliance." Without waiting for his mother's reply, Aladdin opened the street-door, and made the slaves walk out; a white slave followed always by a black one with a basin on his head. When they were all out, the mother followed the last black slave, and he shut the door, full of hope that the sultan, after this present, which was such as he required, would at length receive him as his son-in-law.

The first white slave that went out of the house made all the people, who were going by and saw him, stop; and before they were all out of the house, the streets were crowded with spectators, who ran to see so extraordinary and noble a sight. The dress of each slave was so rich, both from the stuff and the jewels, that those who were dealers in them valued each at no less than a million of money. Besides the neatness and propriety of the dress, the good grace, noble air, and beauty of each slave was unparalleled; their grave walk at an equal distance from each other, the lustre of the jewels, which were large, and curiously set in their girdles of massy gold, and the precious stones in their hats, put the crowds of spectators into such great admiration that they could not weary of gazing at them, and following them with their eyes as far as possible; but the streets were so crowded with people, that none could move out of the spot they stood on. As the procession had to pass through a great many streets to get to the palace, a great part of the city had an opportunity of seeing them. As soon as the first of the slaves arrived at the palace-gate, the porters formed themselves into order, and took him for a king, and were going to kiss the hem of his garment; but the slave, who was instructed by the genie, prevented them, and said, "We are only slaves; our master will appear at the proper time."

Then this slave, followed by the rest, advanced into the second court, which was very spacious, and in which the sultan's household was ranged during the sitting of the divan. The magnificence of the officers, who stood at the head of the troops, was very much eclipsed by the slaves who bore Aladdin's present, of which they themselves made a part. Nothing was ever seen so beautiful and brilliant in the sultan's palace before; and all the lustre of the lords of his court was not to be compared to them.

As the sultan, who had been informed of their coming to the palace, had given orders for them to be admitted when they came, they met with no obstacle, but went into the divan in good order, one part filing to the right, and the other to the left. After they had all entered, and had formed a great semicircle before the sultan's throne, the black slaves laid the basins on the carpet, and all prostrated themselves, touching the carpet with their foreheads, and the white slaves did the same. When they all rose again, the black slaves uncovered the basins, and then all stood with their arms crossed over their breasts.

In the meantime Aladdin's mother advanced to the foot of the throne, and having paid her respects, said to the sultan, "Sir, my son Aladdin is aware that this present, which he has sent your majesty, is much below the Princess Badroulboudour's worth; but hopes, nevertheless, that your majesty will accept it."

The sultan was not able to give the least attention to this compliment of Aladdin's mother. The moment he cast his eyes on the forty basins, brim-full of the most precious, brilliant, and beautiful jewels he had ever seen, and the fourscore slaves, who looked, from the comeliness of their persons and the richness and magnificence of their dress, like so many kings, he was so struck that he could not recover from his admiration; but instead of answering the compliment of Aladdin's mother, addressed himself to the grand vizier, who could no more than the sultan comprehend from whence such a profusion of riches could come. "Well, vizier," said he aloud, "who do you think it can be that has sent me so extraordinary a present? Do you think him worthy of the Princess Badroulboudour, my daughter?"

The vizier, notwithstanding his envy and grief to see a stranger preferred to his son, dared not say so. Aladdin's present was more than sufficient, therefore he returned this answer: "I am so far, sir, from thinking that the person who has made your majesty so noble a present is unworthy of the honour you would do him, that I should be bold to say he deserved much more, if I was not persuaded that the greatest treasure in the world ought not to be put on a level with the princess your majesty's daughter." This advice was applauded by all the lords who were then in council.

The sultan no longer hesitated, nor thought whether Aladdin was endowed with the qualifications requisite in one who aspired to be his son-in-law. The sight alone of such immense riches, and Aladdin's diligence in satisfying his demand without the least difficulty, easily persuaded him that he lacked nothing to render him accomplished, and such as he desired. Therefore, to send Aladdin's mother back with all the satisfaction she could desire, he said to her, "Good woman, go and tell your son that I wait to receive him with open arms, and the more haste he makes to come and receive the princess my daughter from my hands, the greater pleasure he will do me."

As soon as Aladdin's mother retired, over-joyed to see her son raised beyond all expectation to such great honour, the sultan put an end to the audience for that day; and rising from his throne, ordered that the princess's servants should come and carry the basins into their mistress's apartment, whither he went himself to examine them with her at his leisure. The fourscore slaves were not forgotten, but were conducted into the palace; and some time after, the sultan, telling the Princess Badroulboudour of their magnificent appearance, ordered them to be brought before her apartment, that she might see them through the lattice.

In the meantime Aladdin's mother got home, and showed in her face the good news she brought her son. "My son," said she to him, "you have now all the reason in the world to be pleased. Not to keep you too long in suspense, the sultan, with the approbation of the whole court, has declared that you are worthy to marry the Princess Badroulboudour, and waits to embrace you, and arrange your marriage; therefore lose no time in going to him."

Aladdin, charmed with this news, made very little reply, but retired to his room. There, after he had rubbed his lamp, the obedient genie appeared. "Genie," said Aladdin, "I want to bathe immediately, and you must afterwards provide me the richest and most magnificent robe ever worn by a monarch." No sooner were the words out of his mouth, than the genie rendered him, as well as himself, invisible, and transported him into a bath of the finest marble of all sorts of colours; where he was undressed, without seeing by whom, in a neat and spacious hall. From the hall he was led to the bath, and there rubbed and washed with all sorts of scented water. After he had passed through several degrees of heat, he came out, quite a different man from what he was before. When he returned into the hall, he found, instead of his own clothes, a suit the magnificence of which very much surprised him. The genie helped him to dress, and when he had done, transported him back to his own room, where he asked him if he had any other commands. "Yes," answered Aladdin, "I expect you to bring me, as soon as possible, a horse that surpasses in beauty and goodness the best in the sultan's stables, with a saddle, bridle, and harness worth a million of money. I want also twenty slaves, as richly clothed as those who carried the present to the sultan, to walk by my side and follow me, and twenty more to go before me in two ranks. Besides these, bring my mother six women-slaves to wait on her, as richly dressed at least as any of the Princess Badroulboudour's, each loaded with a complete suit fit for any sultaness. I want also ten thousand pieces of gold in ten purses. Go, and make haste."

As soon as Aladdin had given these orders, the genie disappeared and presently returned with the horse, the forty slaves, ten of whom carried each a purse with one thousand pieces of gold, and six women-slaves, each carrying on her head a different dress for Aladdin's mother, wrapped up in a piece of silver stuff, and presented them all to Aladdin.

Of the ten purses Aladdin took but four, which he gave to his mother, telling her that those were to supply her with necessaries; the other six he left in the hands of the slaves who brought them, with an order to throw them by handfuls among the people as they went to the sultan's palace. The six slaves who carried the purses, he ordered likewise to march before him, three on the right hand and three on the left. Afterwards he presented the six women slaves to his mother, telling her they were her slaves, and that the dresses they had brought were for her use.

When Aladdin had thus settled matters, he told the genie he would call for him when he wanted him, and thereupon the genie disappeared. Aladdin's thoughts now were only of answering, as soon as possible, the desire the sultan had shown to see him. He despatched one of the forty slaves to the palace, with an order to address himself to the chief of the officers, to know when he might have the honour to come and throw himself at the sultan's feet. The slave soon acquitted himself of his message, and brought for answer that the sultan waited for him with impatience.

Aladdin immediately mounted his horse, and began his march in the order we have already described; and though he never was on a horse's back before, he rode with such extraordinary grace that the most experienced horseman would not have taken him for a novice. The streets through which he was to pass were almost instantly filled with an enormous crowd of people, who made the air echo with their shouts, especially every time the six slaves who carried the purses threw handfuls of gold into the air on both sides. Those who knew him once when he played in the streets like a vagabond, did not know him again; those who had seen him but a little while before hardly knew him, so greatly were his features altered: such were the effects of the lamp.

Much more attention was paid to Aladdin than to the pomp and magnificence of his attendants, which had been taken notice of the day before, when the slaves walked in procession with the present to the sultan. Nevertheless the horse was very much admired by good judges, who knew how to discern his beauties without being dazzled with the jewels and richness of the harness: and when the report was everywhere spread about that the sultan was going to give the Princess Badroulboudour in marriage to him, nobody thought of his birth, nor envied his good fortune, so worthy he seemed of it.

When he arrived at the palace everything was prepared for his reception; and when he came to the second gate, he would have alighted off his horse, agreeable to the custom observed by the grand vizier, the generals of the armies, and governors of provinces of the first rank; but the chief of the officers who waited on him by the sultan's order prevented him, and attended him to the council-hall, where he helped him to dismount. The officers formed themselves into two ranks at the entrance of the hall. The chief put Aladdin on his right hand, and through the midst of them led him to the sultan's throne.

As soon as the sultan perceived Aladdin, he was surprised to see him more richly and magnificently clothed than ever he had been himself. Besides, he had a certain air of unexpected grandeur, very different from the poverty his mother had appeared in.

But notwithstanding, his surprise did not hinder him from rising off his throne, and descending two or three steps, quick enough to prevent Aladdin's throwing himself at his feet. He embraced him with all the demonstrations of friendship. After this, Aladdin would have cast himself at his feet again; but the sultan held him fast by the hand, and obliged him to sit between him and the grand vizier.

Then Aladdin said, "I receive, sir, the honour which

your majesty out of your great goodness is pleased to confer on me; but permit me to tell you that I have not forgotten that I am your slave; that I know the greatness of your power, and that I am not unaware how much my birth is below the splendour and lustre of the high rank to which I am raised. I ask your majesty's pardon for my rashness, but I cannot dissemble that I should die with grief if I should lose my hope of marrying the princess."

"My son," answered the sultan, embracing him a second time, "you would wrong me to doubt my sincerity for a moment."

After these words the sultan gave a signal, and immediately the air echoed with the sound of trumpets and hautboys, and other musical instruments: and at the same time the sultan led Aladdin into a magnificent hall, where there was prepared a noble feast. The sultan and Aladdin ate by themselves; the grand vizier and the great lords of the court, according to their dignity and rank, waited all the time. The conversation turned on different subjects; but all the while the sultan hardly ever took his eyes off him; and throughout all their conversation Aladdin showed so much good sense, that it confirmed the sultan in the good opinion he had of him.

After the feast, the sultan sent for the chiefjudge of his capital, and ordered him to draw up immediately a contract of marriage between the Princess Badroulboudour, his daughter, and Aladdin.

When the judge had drawn up the contract in all the requisite forms, the sultan asked Aladdin if he would stay in the palace, and solemnise the ceremonies of marriage that day. To which he answered, "Sir, though great is my impatience, yet I beg of you to give me leave to defer it till I have built a palace fit to receive the princess in; I therefore desire you to grant me a convenient spot of ground near your palace, that I may come the more frequently to pay my respects to you, and I will take care to have it finished with all diligence."

"Son," said the sultan, "take what ground you think proper; there is land enough before my palace." After these words he embraced Aladdin again, who took his leave with as much politeness as if he had always lived at court.

Aladdin mounted his horse again, and returned home in the order he came, with the acclamations of the people, who wished him all happiness and prosperity. As soon as he dismounted he retired to his own room, took the lamp, and called the genie as before. "Genie," said Aladdin, "I have had all the reason in the world to commend you hitherto, but now if you have any regard for the lamp your mistress, you must show, if possible, more zeal and diligence than ever. I want you to build me, as soon as you can, a palace at a proper distance from the sultan's, fit to receive my wife the Princess Badroulboudour. I leave the choice of the materials to you, that is to say, porphyry, jasper, agate, lapis lazuli, and the finest marble of the most varied colours; and the style of the building. But in the highest storey of this palace you shall build me a large hall with a dome and four equal fronts; and instead of layers of bricks, the walls shall be made of massy gold and silver, laid alternately; each front shall contain six windows, the lattices of all of which shall be so enriched with diamonds, rubies, and emeralds that they shall exceed everything of the kind that has ever been seen in the world. I would have an inner and outer court before this palace, and a garden, but above all things take care that there be laid in a place, which you shall point out to me, a treasure of gold and silver coin. This palace must be well provided with kitchens and offices, store-houses, and rooms in which to keep choice furniture for every season of the year. I must have stables full of the finest horses, with their equerries and grooms, and hunting equipage. There must be officers to attend the kitchens and offices, and women-slaves to wait on the princess. You understand what I mean, therefore go about it, and come and tell me when all is finished."

By the time Aladdin had instructed the genie with his intentions respecting the building of his palace, the sun was set. The next morning by break of day, Aladdin was no sooner up than the genie presented himself, and said, "Sir, your palace is finished; come and see how you like it." The genie transported him thither in an instant, and he found it so much beyond his expectation that he could not enough admire it. The genie led him through all the apartments, where he met with nothing but what was rich and magnificent, with officers and slaves, all dressed according to their rank and the services to which they were appointed. Then the genie showed him the treasury, which was opened by a treasurer, where Aladdin saw heaps of purses of different sizes, piled up to the top of the ceiling. The genie assured him of the treasurer's fidelity, and thence led him to the stables, where he showed him some of the finest horses in the world, and the grooms busy dressing them. From thence they went to the storehouses, which were filled with all necessary provisions, for both the food and ornament of the horses.

When Aladdin had examined the palace from top to bottom, and particularly the hall with the four-and-twenty windows, and found it much beyond whatever he could have imagined, he said to the genie, "Genie, no one can be better satisfied than I am, and indeed I should be very much to blame if I found any fault. There is only one thing wanting, which I forgot to mention. That is, to lay from the sultan's palace to the door of the apartment designed for the princess, a carpet of fine velvet for her to walk upon." The genie immediately disappeared, and Aladdin saw what he desired executed that minute. Then the genie returned, and carried Aladdin home before the gates of the sultan's palace were opened.

When the porters, who had always been used to an open view, came to open the gates, they were amazed to find it obstructed, and to see a carpet of velvet spread. They did not immediately see what it meant, but when they saw Aladdin's palace distinctly, their surprise was increased. The news of so extraordinary a wonder spread through the palace. The grand vizier, who came soon after the gates were open, was no less amazed than the others, but ran and told the sultan, and endeavoured to make him believe it to be all enchantment. "Vizier," replied the sultan, "why do you say it is enchantment? You know as well as I that it is Aladdin's palace, which I gave him leave to build to receive my daughter in. After the proof we have had of his riches, can we think it strange that he should build a palace in so short a time? He intends to surprise us, and let us see what wonders are to be done with ready money every day.

Confess sincerely to me that that enchantment you talk of proceeds from a little envy."

When Aladdin had been conveyed home, and had dismissed the genie, he found his mother up, and dressing herself in one of the suits that were brought her. By the time the sultan came from the council, Aladdin had prepared his mother to go to the palace with her slaves, and desired her, if she saw the sultan, to tell him she came to do herself the honour of attending the princess towards evening to her palace. Accordingly she went, but though she and the women-slaves who followed her were all dressed like sultanesses, yet the crowd was nothing like so great, because they were all veiled. As for Aladdin, he mounted his horse, and took leave of his paternal house for ever, taking care not to forget his wonderful lamp, and went to the palace with the same pomp as the day before.

As soon as the porters of the sultan's palace saw Aladdin's mother, they went and informed the sultan, who presently ordered the bands of trumpets, cymbals, drums, fifes and hautboys, placed in different parts of the palace, to play and beat, so that the air resounded with sounds which inspired the whole city with joy; the merchants began to adorn their shops and houses with fine carpets and cushions, and bedeck them with boughs, and prepare illuminations for the night. The artists of all sorts left their work, and the people all repaired to the great space between the sultan's and Aladdin's palaces; which last drew all their attention, not only because it was new to them, but because there was no comparison between the two buildings. But they could not imagine by what unheard-of miracle so magnificent a palace could be so soon built, it being apparent to all that there were no prepared materials, or any foundations laid the day before.

Aladdin's mother was received in the palace with honour, and introduced into the Princess Badroulboudour's apartment. As soon as the princess saw her, she went and saluted her, and desired her to sit down on her sofa: and while her women finished dressing her, and adorning her with the jewels with which Aladdin had presented her, a collation was served up. At the same time the sultan, who wanted to be as much with his daughter as possible before he parted with her, came and paid her great respect. The sultan, who had always seen Aladdin's mother dressed very meanly, not to say poorly, was surprised to find her as richly and magnificently clothed as the princess his daughter. This made him think Aladdin equally prudent and wise in whatever he undertook.

When it was night, the princess took leave of the sultan her father, and set out for Aladdin's palace, with his mother on her left hand, followed by a hundred women-slaves, dressed with surprising magnificence. All the bands of music, which played from the time Aladdin's mother arrived, joined together and led the procession. Four hundred of the sultan's young pages carried torches on each side, which, together with the illuminations of the sultan's and Aladdin's palaces, made it as light as day.

At length the princess arrived at the new palace. Aladdin ran with all imaginable joy to receive her at the entrance. His mother had taken care to point him out to the princess, in the midst of the officers that surrounded him, and she was charmed as soon as she saw him. "Adorable princess," said Aladdin to her, saluting her respectfully, "if I have displeased you by my boldness in aspiring to so lovely a princess, and my sultan's daughter, I must tell you that you ought to blame yourself, not me."

"Prince (as I may now call you)," answered the princess, "I am obedient to the will of my father; and it is enough for me to have seen you, to tell you that I obey without reluctance."

Aladdin, charmed with so agreeable and satisfactory an answer, would not keep the princess standing after she had walked so far, but took her by the hand, which he kissed with joy, and led her into a large hall, illuminated with an infinite number of wax candles, where, by the care of the genie, a noble feast was served up. The plates were of massy gold. The vases, basins, and goblets, with which the sideboard was furnished, were gold also, and of exquisite workmanship. The princess, dazzled to see so much riches collected in one place, said to Aladdin, "I thought, Prince, that nothing in the world was so beautiful as the sultan my father's palace; but the sight of this hall alone is enough to show that I was deceived."

Then Aladdin led the princess to the place appointed for her, and as soon as she and his mother were sat down, a band of the most harmonious instruments, accompanied with the voices of beautiful ladies, began a concert, which lasted without intermission to the end of the repast. The princess was so charmed that she declared she never heard anything like it in the sultan her father's court; but she knew not that these musicians were fairies chosen by the genie, slaves of the lamp.

When the supper was ended, and the table taken away, there entered a company of dancers. At length, Aladdin, according to the custom of that time in China, rose up and presented his hand to the Princess Badroulboudour to dance with her, and to finish the ceremonies. They danced with so good a grace that they were the admiration of all the company. Thus ended the ceremonies and rejoicings at the marriage of Aladdin with the Princess Badroulboudour.

PART II

Aladdin and his wife had lived happily after this manner for several years, when the African magician, who undesignedly had been the means of raising him to such good fortune, bethought himself of him in Africa, whither, after his expedition, he had returned. And though he was almost persuaded that Aladdin had died miserably in the subterranean abode where he left him, he had the curiosity to learn about his end with certainty. As he was a great magician, he took out of a cupboard a square covered box, which he made use of in his observations; then sat himself down on his sofa, set it before him, and uncovered it. After he had prepared and levelled the sand which was in it, to discover whether or no Aladdin died in the subterranean abode, he cast the points, drew the figures, and formed a horoscope, by which, when he came to examine it, he found that Aladdin, instead of dying in the cave, had escaped out of it, lived splendidly, was very rich, had married a princess, and was very much honoured and respected.

The magician no sooner understood by the rules of his diabolical art that Aladdin had arrived at that height of good fortune, than a colour came into his face, and he cried out in a rage, "This poor sorry tailor's son has discovered the secret and virtue of the lamp! I believed his death to be certain, but find too plainly he enjoys the fruit of my labour and study! But I will prevent his enjoying it long, or perish in the attempt." The next morning the magician mounted a horse which was in his stable, set out, and stopped only to refresh himself and horse till he arrived at the capital of China. He alighted, took up his lodging in a khan, and stayed there the remainder of the day and the night, to rest after so long a journey.

The next day his first object was to inquire what people said of Aladdin; and, taking a walk through the town, he went to the most public and frequented places, where people of the highest distinction met to drink a certain warm liquor, which he had drunk often when he was there before. As soon as he sat down he was given a glass of it, which he took; but listening at the same time to the discourse of the company on each side of him, he heard them talking of Aladdin's palace. When he had drunk off his glass, he joined them, and taking the opportunity, asked them what palace it was they spoke so well of. "From whence come you?" said the person to whom he addressed himself; "you must certainly be a stranger not to have seen or heard talk of Prince Aladdin's palace (for he was called so after his marriage with the Princess Badroulboudour). I do not say," continued the man, "that it is one of the wonders of the world, but that it is the only wonder of the world; since nothing so grand, rich, and magnificent was ever seen. Certainly you must have come from a great distance, not to have heard of it; it must have been talked of all over the world. Go and see it, and then judge whether I have told you more than the truth."

"Forgive my ignorance," replied the African magician; "I arrived here but yesterday, and came from the furthest part of Africa, where the fame of this palace had not reached when I came away. For the affair which brought me hither was so urgent, that my sole object was to get here as soon as I could, without stopping anywhere, or making any acquaintance. But I will not fail to go and see it; I will go immediately and satisfy my curiosity, if you will do me the favour to show me the way."

The person to whom the African magician addressed himself was pleased to show him the way to Aladdin's palace. When he came to the palace, and had examined it on all sides, he doubted not that Aladdin had made use of the lamp to build it; for he knew that none but the genies, the slaves of the lamp, could have performed such wonders; and piqued to the quick at Aladdin's happiness and greatness, he returned to the khan where he lodged.

The next thing was to learn where the lamp was; if Aladdin carried it about with him, or where he kept it;

and this he was able to discover by an operation of magic. As soon as he entered his lodging, he took his square box of sand, which he always carried with him when he travelled, and after he had performed some operations, he knew that the lamp was in Aladdin's palace, and so great was his joy at the discovery that he could hardly contain himself. "Well," said he, "I shall have the lamp, and I defy Aladdin to prevent my carrying it off and making him sink to his original meanness, from which he has taken so high a flight."

It was Aladdin's misfortune at that time to have gone hunting for eight days, of which only three were past. After the magician had performed the operation which gave him so much joy, he went to the master of the khan, entered into talk with him on indifferent matters, and among the rest, told him he had been to see Aladdin's palace; and added, "and I shall not be easy till I have seen the person to whom this wonderful edifice belongs."

"That will be no difficult matter," replied the master of the khan; "there is not a day passes but he gives an opportunity when he is in town, but at present he is not at home, and has been gone these three days on a hunting-match, which will last eight."

The magician wanted to know no more: he took leave of the master of the khan, and returning to his own chamber, said to himself, "This is an opportunity I ought by no means to let slip." For this purpose he went to a maker and seller of lamps, and asked for a dozen copper lamps: the master of the shop told him he had not so many by him, but if he would have patience till the next day, he would get them for him. The magician appointed this time, and bade him take care that they should be handsome and well polished. After promising to pay him well, he returned to his inn.

The next day the magician called for the twelve lamps, paid the man his full price for them, put them into a basket which he bought on purpose, and with the basket hanging on his arm, went straight to Aladdin's palace; and when he came near it he began crying, "Who will change old lamps for new ones?" As he went along, he gathered a crowd of children about him, who hooted at him, and thought him, as did all who chanced to be passing by, mad or a fool, to offer to change new lamps for old ones.

The African magician never minded all their scoffs and hootings, but still continued crying, "Who will change old lamps for new ones?" He repeated this so often, walking backwards and forwards about the Princess Badroulboudour's palace, that the princess, who was then in the hall with the four-and-twenty windows, hearing a man cry something, and not being able to distinguish his words, by reason of the hooting of the children and increasing mob about him, sent one of her women-slaves down to know what he cried.

It was not long before the slave returned, and ran into the hall, laughing heartily. "Well, giggler," said the princess, "will you tell me what are you laughing at?"

"Madam," answered the slave, laughing still, "who can help laughing to see a fool with a basket on his arm, full of fine new lamps, ask to change them for old ones; the children and mob, crowding about him so that he can hardly stir, make all the noise they can by deriding him."

Another woman-slave, hearing this, said, "Now you speak of lamps, I know not whether the princess has observed it, but there is an old one on the shelf, and whoever owns it will not be sorry to find a new one in its stead. If the princess has a mind she may have the pleasure of trying if this fool is so silly as to give a new lamp for an old one without taking anything for the exchange."

The lamp this slave spoke of was Aladdin's wonderful lamp, which he, for fear of losing, had laid on the shelf before he went hunting, which precaution he had taken several times before, but neither the princess, the slaves, nor the attendants had ever taken any notice of it. At all other times he carried it about with him, and then indeed he might have locked it up, but other people have been guilty of oversights as great, and will be so to the end of time.

The Princess Badroulboudour, who knew not the value of this lamp, and the importance for Aladdin, not to mention herself, of keeping it safe from everybody else, entered into the joke, and bade an attendant take it, and go and make the exchange. The attendant obeyed, went out of the hall, and no sooner got to the palace gates than he saw the African magician, called to him, and showing him the old lamp, said to him, "Give me a new lamp for this."

The magician never doubted but this was the lamp he wanted. There could be no other like it in this palace, where all was gold or silver. He snatched it eagerly out of the man's hand, and thrusting it as far as he could into his breast, offered him his basket, and bade him choose which he liked best. The man picked out one, and carried it to the Princess Badroulboudour, but the exchange was no sooner made than the place rang with the shouts of the children, deriding the magician's folly.

The African magician gave everybody leave to laugh as much as they pleased. He stayed not long about Aladdin's palace, but made the best of his way back without crying any longer "New lamps for old ones." His end was answered, and by his silence he got rid of the children and the mob.

As soon as he got out of the square between the two palaces he skulked down the streets which were the least frequented, and having no more need for his lamps or basket, set them all down in the midst of a street where nobody saw him; then scouring another street or two, he walked till he came to one of the city gates, and pursuing his way through the suburbs, which were very long, he bought some provisions before he left the city, got into the fields, and turned into a road which led to a lonely remote place, where he stopped for a time to execute the design he came about, never thinking about his horse, which he had left at the khan, but considering himself perfectly compensated by the treasure he had acquired.

In this place the African magician passed the remainder of the day, till the darkest time of night, when he pulled the lamp out of his breast and rubbed it. At that summons the genie appeared, and said, "What wouldst thou have? I am ready to obey thee as thy slave, and the slave of all those who have that lamp in their hands, both I and the other slaves of the lamp."

"I command thee," replied the magician, "to transport me immediately and the palace which thou and the other

74

slaves of the lamp have built in this town, just as it is, with all the people in it, to a place in Africa." The genie made no reply, but with the assistance of the other genies, the slaves of the lamp, transported him and the palace entire immediately to Africa, where we will leave the magician, palace, and the Princess Badroulboudour, to speak of the surprise of the sultan.

As soon as the sultan rose the next morning, according to custom, he looked out of the window to have the pleasure of contemplating and admiring Aladdin's palace. But when he first looked that way, and instead of a palace saw an empty space such as it had been before the palace was built, he thought he was mistaken, and rubbed his eyes. He looked again, and saw nothing more the second time than the first, though the weather was fine, the sky clear, and the daybreak had made all objects very distinct. He looked through the two openings on the right and left, and saw nothing more than he had formerly been used to see out of them. His amazement was so great that he stood for some time turning his eyes to the spot where the palace had stood, but where it was no longer to be seen. He could not comprehend how so large a palace as Aladdin's, which he saw plainly every day, and but the day before, should vanish so soon and not leave the least trace behind. "Certainly," said he, to himself, "I am not mistaken. It stood there. If it had tumbled down, the materials would have lain in heaps, and if it had been swallowed up by an earthquake there would be some mark left." Though he was convinced that no palace stood there, he could not help staying there some time, to see whether he might not be mistaken. At last he retired to his apartment, not without looking behind him before he quitted the spot, and ordered the grand vizier to be fetched in all haste, and in the meantime sat down, his mind agitated by many different thoughts.

The grand vizier did not make the sultan wait long for him, but came with so much haste that neither he nor his attendants as they passed by missed Aladdin's palace; neither did the porters, when they opened the palace gates, observe any alteration.

When he came into the sultan's presence, he said to him, "Sir, the haste with which your majesty has sent for me makes me believe something very extraordinary has happened, since you know this is council-day, and I should not fail to attend you there very soon."

"Indeed," said the sultan, "it *is* something very extraordinary, as you say, and you will allow it to be so. Tell me what has become of Aladdin's palace."

"Aladdin's palace!" replied the grand vizier, in great amazement. "I thought, as I passed by, that it stood in its usual place; such substantial buildings are not so easily removed."

"Go to my window," said the sultan, "and tell me if you can see it."

The grand vizier went to the window, where he was struck with no less amazement than the sultan had been. When he was well assured that there was not the least appearance of this palace, he returned to the sultan. "Well," said the sultan, "have you seen Aladdin's palace?"

"Sir," answered the vizier, "your majesty may remember that I had the honour to tell you that that palace, which was the subject of your admiration, with all its immense riches, was only the work of magic and a magician, but your majesty would not pay the least attention to what I said."

The sultan, who could not deny what the grand vizier had represented to him, flew into a great passion. "Where is that impostor, that wicked wretch," said he, "that I may have his head cut off immediately?"

"Sir," replied the grand vizier, "it is some days since he came to take his leave of your majesty; he ought to be sent tc to know what is become of his palace, since he cannot be ignorant of what has been done."

"That is too great a favour," replied the sultan: "go and order a detachment of thirty horse, to bring him to me loaded with chains." The grand vizier went and gave orders for a detachment of thirty horse, and instructed the officer who commanded them how they were to act, that Aladdin might not escape them. The detachment pursued their orders; and about five or six leagues from the town met him returning from hunting. The officer went up to him, and told him that the sultan was so impatient to see him, that he had sent them to accompany him home.

Aladdin had not the least suspicion of the true reason of their meeting him, but pursued his way hunting; but when he came within half a league of the city, the detachment surrounded him, and the officer addressed himself to him, and said, "Prince Aladdin, it is with great regret that I declare to you the sultan's order to arrest you, and to carry you before him as a criminal; I beg of you not to take it ill that we acquit ourselves of our duty, and to forgive us."

Aladdin, who felt himself innocent, was very much

surprised at this declaration, and asked the officer if he knew what crime he was accused of; who replied he did not. Then Aladdin, finding that his retinue was much smaller than this detachment, alighted off his horse, and said to the officer, "Execute your orders; I am not conscious that I have committed any crime against the sultan's person or government." A large long chain was immediately put about his neck, and fastened round his body, so that both his arms were pinioned down; then the officer put himself at the head of the detachment, and one of the troopers took hold of the end of the chain, and proceeding after the officer, led Aladdin, who was obliged to follow him on foot, into the town.

When this detachment entered the suburbs, the people who saw Aladdin thus led as a state criminal, never doubted but that his head was to be cut off; and as he was generally beloved, some took sabres and other arms; and those who had none, gathered stones, and followed the detachment. The last five of the detachment faced about to disperse them; but their number presently increased so much that the detachment began to think that it would be well if they could get into the sultan's palace before Aladdin was rescued; to prevent which, according to the different extent of the streets, they took care to cover the ground by extending or closing. In this manner they arrived at the palace square, and there drew up in a line, and faced about till their officer and the troopers that led Aladdin had got within the gates, which were immediately shut.

Aladdin was carried before the sultan, who waited for him attended by the grand vizier on a balcony; and as soon as he saw him, he ordered the executioner, who waited there on purpose, to cut off his head, without hearing him, or giving him leave to clear himself.

As soon as the executioner had taken off the chain that was fastened about Aladdin's neck and body, and laid down a skin stained with the blood of the many criminals he had executed, he made Aladdin kneel down, and tied a bandage over his eyes. Then drawing his sabre, he prepared to strike the blow by flourishing it three times in the air, waiting for the sultan's signal to separate his head from his body.

At that instant the grand vizier, perceiving that the populace had forced the guard of horse, and crowded the great square before the palace, and were scaling the walls in several places and beginning to pull them down to force their way in, said to the sultan, before he gave the signal, "I beg of your majesty to consider what you are going to do, since you will risk your palace being forced; and who knows what fatal consequences may attend it?"

"My palace forced!" replied the sultan; "who can have such boldness?"

"Sir," answered the grand vizier, "if your majesty will but cast your eyes towards the great square, and on the palace walls, you will know the truth of what I say."

The sultan was so frightened when he saw so great a crowd, and perceived how enraged they were, that he ordered the executioner to put his sabre in the scabbard immediately, and to unbind Aladdin; and at the same time bade the officers declare to the people that the sultan had pardoned him and they might retire.

Then all those who had already got upon the walls and were witnesses of what had passed, got quickly down, overjoyed that they had saved the life of a man they dearly loved, and published the news among the rest, which was presently confirmed by the officers from the top of the terraces. The justice which the sultan had done to Aladdin soon disarmed the populace of their rage; the tumult abated, and the mob dispersed.

When Aladdin found himself at liberty, he turned towards the balcony, and perceiving the sultan, raised his voice, and said to him in a moving manner, "I beg of your majesty to add one favour more to that which I have already received, which is, to let me know my crime."

"Your crime!" answered the sultan: "perfidious wretch! do you not know it? Come up hither, and I will show you."

Aladdin went up, and presented himself to the sultan, who walked in front, without looking at him, saying, "Follow me;" and then led him into his room. When he came to the door, he said, "Go in; you ought to know whereabouts your palace stood; look round, and tell me what has become of it."

Aladdin looked round, but saw nothing. He perceived very well the spot of ground his palace had stood on; but not being able to divine how it had disappeared, this extraordinary and surprising event threw him into such great confusion and amazement that he could not answer one word.

The sultan growing impatient, said to him again, "Where is your palace, and what has become of my daughter?"

Then Aladdin, breaking silence, said to him, "Sir, I see very well, and own that the palace which I have built is not in the place where it was, but is vanished; neither can I tell your majesty where it may be, but I can assure you I have had no hand in it."

"I am not so much concerned about your palace," replied the sultan; "I value my daughter ten thousand times before it, and would have you find her out, otherwise I will cause your head to be struck off, and no consideration shall prevent it."

"I beg your majesty," answered Aladdin, "to grant me forty days to make my inquiries; and if in that time I have not the success I wish for, I will come again and offer my head at the foot of your throne, to be disposed of at your pleasure."

"I give you the forty days you ask for," said the sultan; "but think not to abuse the favour I show you by imagining you shall escape my resentment; for I will find you out in whatsoever part of the world you are."

Aladdin went out of the sultan's presence with great humiliation, and in a condition worthy of pity. He crossed the courts of the palace, hanging down his head, and in such great confusion that he dared not lift up his eyes. The principal officers of the court, who had all professed themselves his friends, and whom he had never disobliged, instead of going up to comfort him, and offer him a refuge in their houses, turned their backs on him to avoid seeing him, lest he should know them. But had they accosted him with a word of comfort or offer of service, they would not have known Aladdin. He did not know himself, and was no longer in his senses, as plainly appeared by his asking everybody he met, at every house, if they had seen his palace, or could tell him any news of it.

These questions made everybody believe that Aladdin was mad. Some laughed at him, but people of sense and humanity, particularly those who had had any connection of business or friendship with him, really pitied him. For three days he rambled about the city after this manner, without coming to any decision, or eating anything, but what some good people forced him to take out of charity.

At last, as he could no longer, in his unhappy condition, stay in a city where he had formerly made so fine a figure, he quitted it, and took the road to the country; and after he had traversed several fields in frightful uncertainty, at the approach of night he came to a riverside. There, possessed by his despair, he said to himself, "Where shall I seek my palace? In what province, country, or part of the world, shall I find that and my dear princess? I shall never succeed; I had better free myself at once from so much fruitless fatigue and such bitter grief." He was just going to throw himself into the river, but, as a good Mussulman, true to his religion, he thought he could not do it without first saying his prayers. Going to prepare himself, he went first to the river-side to wash his hands and face, according to custom. But that place being steep and slippery, owing to the water's beating against it, he slid down, and would certainly have fallen into the river, but for a little rock which projected about two feet out of the earth. Happily also for him, he still had on the ring which the African magician put on his finger before he went down into the subterranean abode to fetch the precious lamp. In slipping down the bank he rubbed the ring so hard, by holding on the rock, that immediately the genie appeared whom he saw in the cave where the magician left him. "What wouldst thou have?" said the genie. "I am ready to obey thee as thy slave, and the slave of all those that have that ring on their finger; both I and the other slaves of the ring."

Aladdin, agreeably surprised at an apparition he so little expected, replied, "Save my life, genie, a second time, either by showing me to the place where the palace I have caused to be built now stands, or by immediately transporting it back to where it first stood."

"What you command me," answered the genie, "is not in my power; I am only the slave of the ring; you must address yourself to the slave of the lamp."

"If it be so," replied Aladdin, "I command thee, by the power of the ring, to transport me to the place where my palace stands, in what part of the world soever it is, and to set me down under the Princess Badroulboudour's window." These words were no sooner out of his mouth than the genie transported him into Africa, to the midst of a large meadow, where his palace stood, a small distance from a great city, and set him exactly under the windows of the princess's apartment, and then left him. All this was done almost in an instant.

Aladdin, notwithstanding the darkness of the night, knew his palace and the Princess Badroulboudour's apartment again very well; but as the night was far advanced, and all was quiet in the palace, he retired to some distance, and sat down at the foot of a large tree. As he had not slept for five or six days, he was not able to resist the drowsiness which came upon him, but fell fast asleep where he was.

The next morning, as soon as the dawn appeared,

Aladdin was agreeably awakened not only by the singing of the birds which had roosted in the tree under which he had passed the night, but of all those which perched in the thick trees of the palace garden. When he cast his eyes on that wonderful building, he felt an inexpressible joy to think he should soon be master of it again, and once more see his dear Princess Badroulboudour. Pleased with these hopes, he immediately got up, went towards the princess's apartment, and walked under her window, in expectation of her rising, that he might see her. Meanwhile, he began to consider with himself from whence his misfortune proceeded; and after mature reflection, he no longer doubted that it was owing to his having put his lamp out of his sight. He accused himself of negligence, and the little care he took of it, to let it be a moment away from him. But what puzzled him most was that he could not imagine who had been so jealous of his happiness. He would soon have guessed this, if he had known that both he and his palace were in Africa, the very name of which would soon have made him remember the magician, his declared enemy; but the genie, the slave of the ring, had not made the least mention of the name of the place, nor had Aladdin asked him.

The Princess Badroulboudour rose earlier that morning than she had done since her transportation into Africa by the magician, whose presence she was forced to endure once a day, because he was master of the palace; but she had always treated him so harshly that he dared not reside in it. As she was dressing, one of the women looking through the window perceived Aladdin, and ran and told her mistress. The princess, who could not believe the news, went herself to the window, and seeing Aladdin, immediately opened it. The noise the princess made in opening the window made Aladdin turn his head that way, and, knowing the princess, he saluted her with an air that expressed his joy. "To lose no time," said she to him, "I have sent to have the private door opened for you; enter, and come up." She then shut the window.

The private door, which was just under the princess's apartment, was soon opened, and Aladdin was conducted up into the princess's room. It is impossible to express their joy at seeing each other after a separation which they both thought was for ever. They embraced several times, and these embracings over, they sat down, shedding tears of joy, and Aladdin said, "I beg you, Princess, before we talk of anything else, to tell me, both for your own sake, the sultan your father's, and mine, what is become of an old lamp which I left upon the shelf in the hall of the four-and-twenty windows, before I went hunting?"

"Alas! dear husband," answered the princess, "I am afraid our misfortune is owing to that lamp: and what grieves me most is that I have been the cause of it."

"Princess," replied Aladdin, "do not blame yourself, since it was entirely my fault, and I ought to have taken more care of it. But let us now think only of repairing the loss; tell me what has happened, and into whose hands it has fallen."

Then the Princess Badroulboudour gave Aladdin an account of how she changed the old lamp for a new one, which she ordered to be fetched, that he might see it, and how the next morning she found herself in the unknown country they were then in, which she was told was Africa by the traitor who had transported her thither by his magic art.

"Princess," said Aladdin, interrupting her, "you have informed me who the traitor is, by telling me we are in Africa. He is the most perfidious of all men; but this is neither the time nor the place to give you a full account of his villainies. I desire you only to tell me what he has done with the lamp, and where he has put it."

"He carries it carefully wrapt up in his bosom," said the princess: "and this I can assure you, because he pulled it out before me, and showed it to me in triumph."

"Princess," said Aladdin, "do not be displeased that I trouble you with so many questions, since they are equally important both to you and me. But tell me, I implore you, how so wicked and perfidious a man treats you."

"Since I have been here," replied the princess, "he comes once a day to see me; and I am persuaded that the little satisfaction he receives from his visits makes him come no oftener. All his discourse tends to persuade me to break that faith I have pledged to you, and to take him for a husband; giving me to understand that I ought not to entertain any hope of ever seeing you again, for that you were dead, and had had your head struck off by the sultan my father's order. He added, to justify himself, that you were an ungrateful wretch; that your good fortune was owing to him, and a great many other things which I forbear to repeat: but, as he received no other answer from me but grievous complaints and tears, he was always forced to retire with as little satisfaction as he came. I doubt not his intention is to allow me time to vanquish my grief, in the hope that I may change my mind; and if I persevere in an obstinate refusal, to use violence. But my dear husband's presence removes all my disquiet."

"I think," replied Aladdin, "I have found means to deliver you from your enemy and mine: to execute this design, it is necessary for me to go to the town. I shall return by noon, and will then communicate my plan to you, and tell you what you must do to ensure success. But that you may not be surprised, I think it proper to tell you that I shall change my apparel, and beg you to give orders that I may not wait long at the private door, but that it may be opened at the first knock," all of which the princess promised to observe.

When Aladdin had got out of the palace by that door, he looked round about him on all sides, and perceiving a peasant going into the country, he hastened after him; and when he had overtaken him, made a proposal to him to change clothes, which the man agreed to. They made the exchange; the countryman went about his business, and Aladdin to the city. After traversing several streets, he came to that part of the town where all sorts of merchants and artisans had their particular streets, according to their trades. He went into that of the druggists; and going into one of the largest and best shops, asked the druggist if he had a certain powder which he named.

The druggist regarding Aladdin from his clothes as very poor, told him he had it, but that it was very dear; upon which Aladdin, penetrating into his thoughts, pulled out his purse, and showing him some gold, asked for half a drachm of the powder, which the druggist weighed, and wrapped up in a piece of paper, and gave him, telling him the price was a piece of gold. Aladdin put the money into his hand, and staying no longer in the town, except just to get a little refreshment, returned to the palace, where he waited not long at the private door. When he came into the princess's apartment, he said to her, "Princess, perhaps the aversion you tell me you have for the magician may hinder your doing what I am going to propose; but give me leave to tell you, it is proper that you should dissemble a little, and do violence to your feelings, if you would deliver yourself from him, and give the sultan your father the satisfaction of seeing you again.

"If you will take my advice," continued he, "dress yourself this moment in one of your richest robes, and when the African magician comes, give him the best reception; receive him with an open countenance, without constraint. From your conversation, let him suppose that you strive to forget me. Invite him to sup with you, and give him to understand you should be glad to taste of some of the best wines of his country. He will go and fetch you some. During his absence, put this powder into one of the cups, and setting it by, charge the slave who attends you to bring you that cup at a signal you shall agree on with her. When the magician and you have eaten and drunk as much as you choose, let her bring you the cup, and change cups with him. He will take it as so great a favour that he will not refuse you, and will drain the cup; but no sooner will he have drunk it off than you will see him fall backwards."

When Aladdin had finished, "I own," answered the

princess, "I shall do myself great violence in consenting to make the magician such advances as I see are absolutely necessary for me to make; but what cannot one resolve to do against a cruel enemy? I will therefore follow your advice." After the princess had agreed to the measures proposed by Aladdin, he took his leave of her, and went and spent the rest of the day in the neighbourhood of the palace till it was night, when he might safely return to the private door.

The Princess Badroulboudour, who was inconsolable at being separated not only from her dear husband, but also from the sultan her father, had, ever since that cruel separation, lived in great neglect of her person. She had almost forgotten to keep herself neat, particularly after the first time the magician paid her a visit; for she learned from some of the women, who knew him again, that it was he who took the old lamp in exchange for a new one, which notorious cheat rendered the sight of him more abhorrent. However, the opportunity of punishing him as he deserved made her resolve to gratify Aladdin. As soon, therefore, as he was gone, she sat down at her toilet, and was dressed by her women to the best advantage, in the richest robes. Her girdle was of the finest and largest diamonds set in gold, which she matched with a necklace of pearls, six on a side, so well setting off the one in the middle, which was the largest and most valuable, that the greatest sultanesses and queens would have been proud to be adorned with only two of the smallest. Her bracelets were of diamonds and rubies intermixed.

When the Princess Badroulboudour was completely dressed, she consulted her glass and her women as to how she looked, and when she found she would easily be able to flatter the foolish magician, she sat down on a sofa, awaiting his arrival.

The magician came at the usual hour, and as soon as he entered the great hall, where the princess waited to receive him, she rose up and pointed with her hand to the most honourable place, waiting till he sat down, that she might sit at the same time, which was a piece of civility she had never shown him before.

The African magician was very much surprised. The majestic and graceful air with which she received him, so opposed to her former behaviour, quite bewildered him.

When he had sat down, the princess, to free him from his embarrassment, broke silence first, and said, "You are doubtless amazed to find me so much altered to-day from what I used to be; but your surprise will not be so great when I tell you that I am naturally of a disposition so opposed to melancholy and grief, sorrow and uneasiness, that I always strive to put them as far away as possible when I find the reason of them is past. I have reflected on what you told me of Aladdin's fate, and know the sultan my father's temper so well that I am persuaded that Aladdin could not escape the terrible effects of his rage; therefore, should I continue to lament him all my life, my tears cannot recall him. To begin to cast off all melancholy, I am resolved to banish it entirely; and, persuaded you will bear me company to-night, I have ordered a supper to be prepared; but as I have no wines except those of China, I have a great desire to taste the African wine, and doubt not you will get some of the best."

The African magician, who had looked upon the happiness of coming so soon and so easily into the Princess Badroulboudour's good graces as impossible, could not think of words enough to express his gratitude: but to put an end the sooner to a conversation which would have embarrassed him, he turned it upon the wines of Africa, and said, "Of all the advantages Africa can boast, that of producing the most excellent wines is one of the principal. I have a vessel of seven years old, which has never been broached; and it is indeed not praising it too much to say that it is the finest wine in the world. If my princess," added he, "will give me leave, I will go and fetch two bottles, and return again immediately."

"I should be sorry to give you that trouble," replied the princess; "you had better send for them."

"It is necessary I should go myself," answered the African magician; "for nobody but myself knows where the key of the cellar is laid, or has the secret to unlock the door."

"If it be so," said the princess, "make haste back again; for the longer you stay, the greater will be my impatience, and we shall sit down to supper as soon as you come back."

The African magician, full of hope, flew rather than ran, and returned quickly with the wine. The princess, not doubting in the least but that he would make haste, put with her own hand the powder Aladdin gave her into the cup that was set apart for that purpose. They sat down at the table opposite to each other, the magician's back towards the sideboard. The princess presented him with the best on the table, and said to him, "If it pleases you, I will entertain you with a concert of vocal and instrumental music; but, as we are only two, I think conversation may be more agreeable." This the magician took as a new favour.

After they had eaten some time, the princess called for some wine, and drank the magician's health; and afterwards said to him, "Indeed you were right to commend your wine, since I never tasted any so delicious in my life."

"Charming princess," said he, holding in his hand the cup which had been presented to him, "my wine becomes more exquisite by your approbation of it."

"Then drink my health," replied the princess; "you will find I understand wines." He drank the princess's health, and returning the cup, said, "I think myself happy, princess, that I reserved this wine for so good an occasion; and I own I never before drank any so excellent in every respect."

Presently, the princess, who had completely charmed the African magician by her civility and obliging behaviour, gave the signal to the slave who served them with wine, bidding her bring the cup which had been filled for herself, and at the same time bring the magician a full cup. When they both had their cups in their hands, she presented to him the cup which was in her hand, and held out her hand to receive his. He for his part hastened to make the exchange with the greater pleasure because he looked upon this favour as the most certain token of an entire conquest over the princess, which raised his happiness to its height. Before he drank, he said to her, with the cup in his hand, "Indeed, I shall never, lovely princess, forget my recovering, by drinking out of your cup, that life which your cruelty, had it continued, would have made me despair of."

The Princess Badroulboudour, who began to be tired of this barefaced foolishness of the African magician, interrupted him, and said, "Let us drink first, and then say what you will afterwards;" and at the same time set the cup to her lips, while the African magician, who was eager to get his wine off first, drank up the very last drop. Then he fell backwards lifeless.

The princess had no occasion to order the back-door to be opened to Aladdin; for her women were so arranged from the great hall to the foot of the staircase, that the word was no sooner given that the African magician was fallen backwards than the door was opened that instant.

As soon as Aladdin entered the hall, he saw the magician stretched backwards on the sofa. The Princess Badroulboudour rose from her seat, and ran overjoyed to embrace him; but he stopped her, and said, "Princess, it is not yet time; oblige me by retiring to your apartment, and let me be left alone a moment, while I endeavour to transport you back to China as quickly as you were brought from thence."

When the princess, her women and attendants, had gone out of the hall, Aladdin shut the door, and going to the dead body of the magician, opened his vest, and took out the lamp carefully wrapt up; and on his unfolding and rubbing it, the genie immediately appeared. "Genie," said Aladdin, "I command thee, on the part of thy good mistress this lamp, to transport this palace directly into China." The genie bowed his head in token of obedience, and disappeared. Immediately the palace was transported into China, and its removal was only felt by two little shocks, the one when it was lifted up, the other when it was set down, and both in a very short interval of time.

Aladdin went down to the princess's apartment, and embracing her, said, "I can assure you, princess, that your joy and mine will be complete to-morrow morning." The princess, who had not quite finished supper, guessed that Aladdin might be hungry, and ordered the meats that were served up in the great hall, and were scarcely touched, to be brought down. The princess and Aladdin ate as much as they thought fit, and drank in like manner of the African magician's old wine; then they retired to rest.

From the time of the transportation of Aladdin's palace, and of the Princess Badroulboudour in it, the sultan, that princess's father, was inconsolable. He hardly slept night or day, and instead of taking measures to avoid everything that could keep up his affliction, he indulged it; he went now many times in the day to renew his tears, and plunged himself into the deepest melancholy.

The very morning of the return of Aladdin's palace, the sultan went, at break of day, into his room to indulge his sorrows. Centred in himself, and in a pensive mood, he cast his eyes in a melancholy manner towards the place where he remembered the palace once stood, expecting only to see an open space. Perceiving that vacancy filled up, he at first imagined it to be the effect of a fog; but looking more attentively, he was convinced beyond the power of doubt that it was his son-in-law's palace. Then joy and gladness succeeded to sorrow and grief. He immediately ordered a horse to be saddled, which he mounted that instant, thinking he could not make haste enough to get to Aladdin's palace.

Aladdin, who foresaw what would happen, rose that morning by daybreak, put on one of the most magnificent robes his wardrobe afforded, and went up into the hall of twenty-four windows, from whence he perceived the sultan coming, and got down soon enough to receive him at the foot of the great staircase, and to help him to dismount. "Aladdin," said the sultan, "I cannot speak to you till I have seen and embraced my daughter."

He led the sultan into the Princess Badroulboudour's apartment. She had been told by him when he rose that she was no longer in Africa, but in China, and in the capital of the sultan her father. The sultan embraced her with his face bathed in tears of joy.

At last the sultan broke silence, and said, "You have undergone a great deal; for a large palace cannot be so suddenly transported, as yours has been, without great fright and terrible anguish. Tell me all that has happened, and conceal nothing from me."

The princess, who took great pleasure in complying, gave the sultan a full account of how the African magician disguised himself like a seller of lamps, and offered to change new lamps for old ones; and how she amused herself in making that exchange, being entirely ignorant of the secret and importance of the lamp; how the palace and herself were carried away and transported into Africa, with the African magician, who was recollected by two of her women when he had the boldness to pay her the first visit after the success of his audacious enterprise, to propose that she should marry him; how he persecuted her till Aladdin's arrival; how he and she concerted measures together to get the lamp again, which he carried about him, and the success they had; and how she had invited him to supper, and had given him the cup with the powder, prepared for him. "For the rest," added she, "I leave it to Aladdin to give you an account."

Aladdin had not much to tell the sultan, but only said, "When the private door was opened, I went into the great hall, where I found the magician lying dead on the sofa. As soon as I was alone, and had taken the lamp out of the magician's breast, I made use of the same secret as he had done to remove the palace, and carry off the princess; and by that means the palace was brought into the same place where it stood before; and I have the happiness to bring back the princess to your majesty, as you commanded me. But that your majesty may not think that I impose upon you, if you will go up into the hall, you shall see the magician, punished as he deserved."

The sultan, to be assured of the truth, rose up instantly, and went up into the hall, and when he saw the African magician dead, he embraced Aladdin with great tenderness, and said, "My son, be not displeased at my proceedings against you; they arose from my love for my daughter, and therefore you ought to forgive the excesses to which it hurried me."

"Sir," replied Aladdin, "I have not the least reason to complain of your majesty's conduct, since you did nothing but what your duty required of you. This infamous magician, the basest of men, was the sole cause of my misfortune. When your majesty has leisure, I will give you an account of another villainous action he was guilty of to me, which was no less black and base than this, from which I was preserved in a very strange manner."

"I will take an opportunity, and that very shortly," replied the sultan, "to hear it; but in the meantime let us think only of rejoicing, and the removal of this odious object."

Aladdin ordered the magician's dead carcass to be removed. In the meantime the sultan commanded the drums, trumpets, cymbals, and other instruments of music to sound, and a feast of ten days to be proclaimed for joy at the return of the Princess Badroulboudour, and Aladdin with his palace.

Thus Aladdin escaped a second time the danger of losing his life.

But the African magician had a younger brother, who was as great a necromancer, and even surpassed him in villainy and pernicious designs. As they did not live together, or in the same city, but oftentimes when one was in the east the other was in the west, they each failed not every year to discover by their art where the other was, and whether he stood in need of any assistance.

Some time after the African magician had failed in his enterprise against Aladdin's happiness, his younger brother, who had not heard any tidings of him for a year, and was not in Africa, but in a distant country, was anxious to know in what part of the world he was, how he did, and what he was doing; and as he, as well as his brother, always carried a geomantic square instrument about with him, he prepared the sand, cast the points, and drew the figures. On examining the "houses" he found that his brother was no longer living, that he had been poisoned, and died suddenly; that it had happened in the capital of the kingdom of China, and that the person who had poisoned him was of low birth, and married to a princess, a sultan's daughter.

When the magician had after this manner learned his brother's fate, he lost no time in useless regret, which could not restore him to life again, but resolving immediately to avenge his death, he took horse, and set out for China, where, after crossing plains, rivers, mountains, deserts, and a long tract of country, without stopping, he arrived after incredible fatigue.

When he came to the capital of China, which his knowledge of geomancy pointed out to him, he took a lodging. The next day he went out and walked through the town, not so much to observe its beauties, to which he was indifferent, as to take proper measures to execute his pernicious design. He went into the most frequented places, where he listened to everybody's conversation. In a place where people went to play at all sorts of games, he heard some persons talking of the virtue and piety of a woman called Fatima, who had retired from the world, and of the miracles she performed. As he fancied that this woman might be serviceable to him for the project he had in his head, he took one of the company aside, and desired him to tell him more particularly who this holy woman was, and what sort of miracles she performed.

"What!" said the person whom he addressed, "have you never seen or heard of her? She is the admiration of the whole town, for her fasting, her austerities, and her exemplary life. Except on Mondays and Fridays, she never stirs out of her little cell; and the days on which she comes into the town she does an infinite deal of good; for there is not a person who has the headache who is not cured by her laying her hand upon him."

The magician wanted no further information. He only asked in what part of the town this holy woman's cell was. After he had been told, he determined on a detestable design; watched her steps the first day she went out after he had made this enquiry, and never lost sight of her till evening, when he saw her re-enter her cell. Then he went to one of those houses where they sell a certain hot liquor, and where any person may pass the night, particularly during the great heats, when the people of that country prefer lying on a mat to going to bed. About midnight, after the magician had paid the master of the house for what little he had called for, he went direct to the cell of Fatima, the holy woman. He had no difficulty in opening the door, which was only fastened with a latch, and he shut it again after he had got in, without any noise. When he entered the cell he perceived Fatima in the moonlight lying on a sofa covered only by an old mat, with her head leaning against the wall. He awakened her, and clapped a dagger to her breast.

Poor Fatima, opening her eyes, was very much surprised to see a man with a dagger at her breast ready to stab her. "If you cry out," he said, "or make the least noise, I will kill you; but get up and do as I bid you."

Fatima, who had lain down in her clothes, got up, trembling with fear. "Do not be so frightened," said the magician; "I only want your gown: give it me at once, and take mine." Accordingly Fatima and he changed clothes. Then he said, "Colour my face as yours is, that I may look like you;" but perceiving that the poor creature

99

could not help trembling, he said, "I tell you again, you need not fear anything; I will not take away your life." Fatima lighted her lamp, and made him come into the cell; and taking a pencil, and dipping it in a certain liquor, she rubbed it over his face and assured him that the dye would not change, and that his face was of the same colour as her own; after which, she put her own head-dress on his head, with a veil, with which she showed him how to hide his face as he passed through the town. After this, about his neck she put a long string of beads, which hung down to his waist, and, giving him the stick she was accustomed to walk with, she brought him a looking-glass, and bade him see if he were not as like her as possible. The magician found himself as much disguised as he wished to be; but he did not keep the promise he so solemnly gave to the good Fatima, for he killed her at once.

The magician, thus disguised like the holy woman, spent the remainder of the night in the cell. The next morning, two hours after sunrise, though it was not the day the holy woman used to go out, he crept out of the cell, being well persuaded that nobody would ask him any question about it; or, if they should, he had an answer ready for them. As one of the first things he had done after his arrival was to find out Aladdin's palace, he went straight thither.

As soon as the people saw the holy woman, as they imagined him to be, they gathered about him in a great crowd. Some begged his blessing, others kissed his hand, and some, more reserved, only the hem of his garment; while others, if their heads ached, or they desired to be preserved against headache, stooped for him to lay his hands upon them; which he did, muttering some words in form of a prayer. In short, he counterfeited so well that everybody took him for the holy woman.

After stopping frequently to satisfy these people, who received neither good nor harm from his imposition of hands, he came at last to the square before Aladdin's palace. The crowd was so great that the eagerness to get at him increased in proportion. Those who were the most zealous and strong forced their way through the crowd to get near. There were such quarrels and so great a noise that the princess, who was in the hall of the four-and-twenty windows, heard it, and asked what was the matter; but nobody being able to give an account, she ordered them to go and see. One of her women looked out of a window, and told her that a great crowd of people was gathered about the holy woman, to be cured of the headache by the imposition of her hands.

The princess, who had for a long time heard a great deal of this holy woman, but had never seen her, felt great curiosity to have some conversation with her, and immediately sent four chamberlains for the pretended holy woman.

As soon as the crowd saw the chamberlains coming, they made way, and the magician advanced to meet them, overjoyed to find his plot work so well. "Holy woman," said one of the officers, "the princess wants to see you, and has sent us for you."

"The princess does me too great an honour," replied the false Fatima, "but I am ready to obey her command," and he followed the chamberlains into the palace.

When the magician, who under a holy garment disguised such a wicked heart, was introduced into the great hall, and perceived the princess, he began a prayer, which contained a long enumeration of vows and good wishes for the princess's health and prosperity, and that she might have everything she desired. Then he displayed all his deceitful, hypocritical rhetoric, to insinuate himself into the princess's favour under the cloak of piety, which it was no hard matter for him to do; for as the princess herself was naturally good, she was easily persuaded that all the world was like her, especially those who made profession of serving God in solitary retreat.

When the pretended Fatima had made an end of his long harangue, the princess said to him, "I thank you, good mother, for your prayers. Come and sit by me." The false Fatima sat down with affected modesty: then the princess said, "My good mother, I have one thing to ask you, which you must not refuse me; which is, to stay with me, that you may teach me your way of living, and that I may learn from your good example."

"Princess," said the counterfeit Fatima, "I beg of you not to ask what I cannot consent to, without neglecting my prayers and devotions."

"That shall be no hindrance to you," answered the princess. "I have a great many apartments unoccupied; you shall choose which you like best, and shall have as much liberty to perform your devotions as if you were in your own cell."

The magician, who wanted nothing better than to introduce himself into Aladdin's palace, where it would be a much easier matter for him to execute his pernicious design, under the favour and protection of the princess, than if he had been forced to come and go from the cell to the palace, did not urge much to excuse himself from accepting the obliging offer the princess made him. "Princess," said he, "whatever resolutions a poor wretched woman, such as I am, may have made to renounce the pomp and grandeur of this world, I dare not presume to oppose the will and command of so pious and charitable a princess."

Upon this the princess rose up and said, "Come along with me, I will show you what empty apartments I have, that you may make choice of those which you like best." The magician followed the Princess Badroulboudour, and made choice of that which was the most poorly furnished, saying, "It is too good for me; I only accept it to please you."

Then the princess wished to take him back again into the great hall to dine with her; but considering that then he would be obliged to show his face, which he had all the time taken care to hide, and fearing that the princess might find out that he was not Fatima, he begged her earnestly to dispense with him, telling her that he never ate anything but bread and dried fruits, and that he desired to eat a slight repast in his own room. This the princess granted him, saying, "You may be as free here, good mother, as if you were in your own cell. I will order you a dinner, but, remember, I shall expect you as soon as you have finished."

After the princess had dined, the false Fatima failed not to wait upon her. "My good mother," said the princess, "I am overjoyed to have the company of so holy a woman as yourself, who will confer a blessing

103

upon this palace. But now that I am speaking of this palace, pray how do you like it? And before I show you the rest, tell me first what you think of this hall."

At this question the counterfeit Fatima, who, to act his part the better, pretended to hang down his head, without so much as ever once lifting it, at last looked up; and, surveying the hall from one end to the other, he said to the princess, "As far as such a solitary being as I can judge, this hall is truly admirable and most beautiful; it lacks but one thing."

"What is that, good mother?" answered the Princess Badroulboudour, "tell me, I implore you. For my part, I have always believed and have heard that it lacked nothing; but if it does, that want shall be supplied."

"Princess," said the false Fatima, with great dissimulation, "forgive me for the liberty I have taken; but if my opinion can be of any importance, it is that if a roc's egg were hung up in the middle of the dome, this hall would have no parallel in the four quarters of the world, and your palace would be the wonder of the universe."

"My good mother," said the princess, "what is a roc, and where could I get an egg?"

"Princess," replied the pretended Fatima, "it is a bird of prodigious size, which inhabits the top of Mount Caucasus; the architect who built your palace can get you one."

After the Princess Badroulboudour had thanked the false Fatima for what she believed her good advice, she conversed with her upon other matters, but she could not forget the roc's egg, of which she determined to tell Aladdin when he returned from hunting. He had been gone six days, which the magician knew, and therefore took advantage of his absence. But he returned that evening after the false Fatima had taken leave of the princess, and retired to his room. As soon as he arrived, Aladdin went straight up to the princess's apartment, and saluted and embraced her. She seemed to receive him coldly. "My princess," said he, "I think you are not so cheerful as usual. Has anything happened during my absence to give you any trouble or dissatisfaction? If so, do not conceal it from me. I will leave nothing undone that is in my power to please you."

"It is a trifling matter," replied the princess, "which gives me so little concern that I should not have thought you would perceive it in my countenance. But since you have unexpectedly discovered it, I will no longer disguise a matter of so little consequence from you.

"I always believed, as you did," continued the Princess Badroulboudour, "that our palace was the most superb, magnificent, and complete one in the world, but I will tell you now what I find fault with upon examining the hall of four-and-twenty windows. Do you not think, with me, that it would be better if a roc's egg were hung up in the midst of the dome?"

"Princess," replied Aladdin, "it is enough that you think it needs such a thing. You shall see by my diligence that there is nothing which I would not do for your sake."

Aladdin left the Princess Badroulboudour that very moment, and went up into the hall of four-and-twenty windows. Pulling out of his bosom the lamp, which, after the danger he had been exposed to, he always carried about with him, he rubbed it, upon which the genie immediately appeared. "Genie," said Aladdin, "there ought to be a roc's egg hung up in the midst of the dome. I command thee, in the name of this lamp, to repair the deficiency."

Aladdin had no sooner pronounced these words than the genie gave so loud and terrible a cry that the hall shook, and Aladdin could scarcely stand upright. "What? wretch," said the genie, in a voice that would have made the most undaunted man tremble, "is it not enough that I and my companions have done everything for you, that you, with unheard-of ingratitude, must command me to bring my master, and hang him up in the midst of this dome? This attempt deserves that you, your wife, and your palace should be immediately reduced to ashes. You are fortunate, however, in not being the real author of this request. It does not come from yourself. Know, then, that the true author is the brother of the African magician, your enemy, whom you have destroyed as he deserved. He is now in your palace, disguised in the clothes of the holy woman Fatima, whom he has murdered, and it is he who has suggested to your wife to make this pernicious demand. His design is to kill you, therefore take care of yourself." After these words the genie disappeared.

Aladdin lost not a word of what the genie had said. He had heard of the holy woman Fatima, and how she could cure the headache. He returned to the princess's apartment, and without mentioning a word of what had happened, he sat down, and complained of a great pain which had suddenly seized his head. Upon this the princess immediately ordered the holy woman to be fetched, and then told Aladdin how she had come to the palace.

When the pretended Fatima came, Aladdin said, "Come hither, good mother; I am glad to see you here at so fortunate a time. I am tormented with a violent pain in my head, and request your assistance. I hope you will not refuse me that kindness which you have done to so many persons afflicted with the headache." So saying, he rose up, but held down his head.

The counterfeit Fatima advanced towards him, with his hand all the time on a dagger, concealed in his girdle under his gown. Aladdin saw this, and, seizing his hand, pierced him to the heart with his own dagger, and then threw him down on the floor dead.

"My dear husband, what have you done?" cried the princess in surprise. "You have killed the holy woman!"

"No, my princess," answered Aladdin, without emotion, "I have not killed Fatima, but a wicked wretch that would have assassinated me, if I had not prevented him. This wicked man," added he, uncovering his face, "has strangled Fatima, whom you accuse me of killing, and disguised himself in her clothes, to come and murder me. He is the brother of the African magician." Then Aladdin told her how he came to know these particulars, and afterwards ordered the dead body to be taken away.

Thus was Aladdin delivered from the persecution of the two magicians. Within a few years afterwards, the sultan died in a good old age, and the Princess Badroulboudour, as lawful heir of the crown, succeeded him. She shared her power with Aladdin, and they reigned together many years, and left a numerous and illustrious posterity behind them.

PART TWO

SINBAD

THE FIRST VOYAGE OF
SINBAD THE SAILOR

My father left me a considerable estate, the best part of which I spent in riotous living during my youth; but I perceived my error, and reflected that riches were perishable, and quickly consumed by such ill managers as myself. I further considered that by my irregular way of living I had wretchedly misspent my time, which is the most valuable thing in the world. Struck with those reflections, I collected the remains of my furniture, and sold all my patrimony by public auction to the highest bidder. Then I entered into a contract with some merchants, who traded by sea: I took the advice of such as I thought most capable to give it me; and resolving to improve what money I had, I went to Balsora, and embarked with several merchants on board a ship which we jointly fitted out.

We set sail, and steered our course towards the East Indies, through the Persian Gulf, which is formed by the coasts of Arabia Felix on the right, and by those of Persia on the left, and, according to common opinion, is seventy leagues across at the broadest part. The eastern sea, as well as that of the Indies, is very spacious: it is bounded on one side by the coasts of Abyssinia, and is 4,500 leagues in length to the isles of Vakvak. At first I was troubled with sea-sickness, but speedily recovered my health, and was not afterwards troubled with that disease.

In our voyage we touched at several islands, where we sold or exchanged our goods. One day, whilst under sail, we were becalmed near a little island, almost even with the surface of the water, which resembled a green meadow. The captain ordered his sails to be furled, and permitted such persons as had a mind to do so to land upon the island, amongst whom I was one.

But while we were diverting ourselves with eating and drinking, and recovering ourselves from the fatigue of the sea, the island on a sudden trembled, and shook us terribly.

They perceived the trembling of the island on board the ship, and called us to re-embark speedily, or we should all be lost, for what we took for an island was only the back of a whale. The nimblest got into the sloop, others betook themselves to swimming; but for my part I was still upon the back of the whale when he dived into the sea, and had time only to catch hold of a piece of wood that we had brought out of the ship to make a fire. Meanwhile, the captain, having received those on board who were in the sloop, and taking up some of those that swam, resolved to use the favourable gale that had just risen, and hoisting his sails, pursued his voyage, so that it was impossible for me to regain the ship.

Thus was I exposed to the mercy of the waves, and struggled for my life all the rest of the day and the following night. Next morning I found my strength gone, and despaired of saving my life, when happily a wave threw me against an island. The bank was high and rugged, so that I could scarcely have got up had it not been for some roots of trees, which fortune seemed to have preserved in this place for my safety. Being got up, I lay down upon the ground half dead until the sun appeared; then, though I was very feeble, both by reason of my hard labour and want of food, I crept along to look for some herbs fit to eat, and had the good luck not only to find some, but likewise a spring of excellent water, which contributed much to restore me. After this I advanced farther into the island, and came at last into a fine plain, where I perceived a horse feeding at a great distance. I went towards him, between hope and fear, not knowing whether I was going to lose my life or save it. Presently I heard the voice of a man from under ground, who immediately appeared to me, and asked who I was. I gave him an account of my adventure; after which, taking me by the hand, he led me into a cave, where there were several other people, no less amazed to see me than I was to see them.

I ate some victuals which they offered me, and then asked them what they did in such a desert place. They answered that they were grooms belonging to King Mihrage, sovereign of the island, and that every year they brought thither the king's horses. They added that they were to get home to-morrow, and had I been one day later I must have perished, because the inhabited part of the island was at a great distance, and it would have been impossible for me to have got thither without a guide.

Next morning they returned with their horses to the capital of the island, took me with them, and presented me to King Mihrage. He asked me who I was, and by what adventure I came into his dominions. And, after I had satisfied him, he told me he was much concerned for my misfortune, and at the same time ordered that I should want for nothing, which his officers were so generous and careful as to see exactly fulfilled.

Being a merchant, I frequented the society of men of my own profession, and particularly inquired for those who were strangers, if perhaps I might hear any news from Bagdad, or find an opportunity to return thither, for King Mihrage's capital was situated on the edge of the sea, and had a fine harbour, where ships arrived daily from the different quarters of the world. I frequented also the society of the learned Indians, and took delight in hearing them discourse; but withal I took care to make my court regularly to the king, and conversed with the governors and petty kings, his tributaries, that were about him. They asked me a thousand questions about my country, and I, being willing to inform myself as to their laws and customs, asked them everything which I thought worth knowing.

There belonged to this king an island named Cassel. They assured me that every night a noise of drums was heard there, whence the mariners fancied that it was the residence of Degial. I had a great mind to see this wonderful place, and on my way thither saw fishes of one hundred and two hundred cubits long, that occasion more fear than hurt, for they are so timid that they will fly at the rattling of two sticks or boards. I saw likewise other fishes, about a cubit in length, that had heads like owls.

As I was one day at the port after my return, a ship arrived, and as soon as she cast anchor, they begun to unload her, and the merchants on board ordered their goods to be carried into the warehouse. As I cast my eye upon some bales, and looked at the name, I found my own, and perceived the bales to be the same that I had embarked at Balsora. I also knew the captain; but being persuaded that he believed me to be drowned, I went and asked him whose bales they were. He replied: "They belonged to a merchant of Bagdad, called Sinbad, who came to sea with us; but one day, being near an island, as we thought, he went ashore with several other passengers upon this supposed island, which was only a monstrous whale that lay asleep upon the surface of the water; but as soon as he felt the heat of the fire they had kindled on his back to dress some victuals he began to move, and dived under water: most of the persons who were upon him perished, and among them unfortunate Sinbad. Those bales belonged to him, and I am resolved to trade with them until I meet with some of his family, to whom I may return the profit."

"Captain," said I, "I am that Sinbad whom you thought to be dead, and those bales are mine."

When the captain heard me speak thus, "O heaven," said he, "whom can we ever trust now-a-days? There is no faith left among men. I saw Sinbad perish with my own eyes, and the passengers on board saw it as well as I, and yet you tell me you are that Sinbad. What impudence is this! To look at you, one would take you to be a man of honesty, and yet you tell a horrible falsehood, in order to possess yourself of what does not belong to you."

"Have patience, captain," replied I; "do me the favour to hear what I have to say."

"Very well," said he, "speak; I am ready to hear you." Then I told him how I escaped, and by what adventure I met with the grooms of King Mihrage, who brought me to his court.

He was soon persuaded that I was no cheat, for there came people from his ship who knew me, paid me great compliments, and expressed much joy to see me alive. At last he knew me himself, and embracing me, "Heaven be praised," said he, "for your happy escape; I cannot enough express my joy for it: there are your goods; take and do with them what you will." I thanked him, acknowledged his honesty, and in return offered him part of my goods as a present, which he generously refused.

I took out what was most valuable in my bales, and presented it to King Mihrage, who, knowing my misfortune, asked me how I came by such rarities. I acquainted him with the whole story. He was mightily pleased at my good luck, accepted my present, and gave me one much more considerable in return. Upon this I took leave of him, and went aboard the same ship, after I had exchanged my goods for the commodities of that country. I carried with me wood of aloes, sandal, camphor, nutmegs, cloves, pepper, and ginger. We passed by several islands, and at last arrived at Balsora, from whence I came to this city, with the value of one hundred thousand sequins. My family and I received one another with transports of sincere friendship. I bought slaves and fine lands, and built me a great house. And thus I settled myself, resolving

to forget the miseries I had suffered, and to enjoy the
pleasures of life.

THE SECOND VOYAGE OF
SINBAD THE SAILOR

I designed, after my first voyage, to spend the rest of
my days at Bagdad; but it was not long ere I grew
weary of a quiet life. My inclination to trade revived.
I bought goods suited to the commerce I intended, and
put to sea a second time, with merchants of known
probity. We embarked on board a good ship, and after
recommending ourselves to God, set sail. We traded
from island to island, and exchanged commodities with
great profit. One day we landed on an island covered
with several sorts of fruit trees, but so unpeopled, that
we could see neither man nor beast upon it. We went
to take a little fresh air in the meadows, and along
the streams that watered them. Whilst some diverted
themselves with gathering flowers, and others with
gathering fruits, I took my wine and provisions, and
sat down by a stream betwixt two great trees, which
formed a curious shape. I made a very good meal, and
afterwards fell asleep. I cannot tell how long I slept, but
when I awoke the ship was gone.

I was very much surprised to find the ship gone. I got
up and looked about everywhere, and could not see one

117

of the merchants who landed with me. At last I perceived the ship under sail, but at such a distance that I lost sight of her in a very little time.

I leave you to guess at my melancholy reflections in this sad condition. I was ready to die with grief: I cried out sadly, beat my head and breast, and threw myself down upon the ground, where I lay some time in a terrible agony. I upbraided myself a hundred times for not being content with the produce of my first voyage, that might well have served me all my life. But all this was in vain, and my repentance out of season.

At last I resigned myself to the will of God; and not knowing what to do, I climbed up to the top of a great tree, from whence I looked about on all sides to see if there was anything that could give me hope. When I looked towards the sea, I could see nothing but sky and water, but looking towards the land I saw something white; and, coming down from the tree, I took up what provision I had left and went towards it, the distance being so great that I could not distinguish what it was.

When I came nearer, I thought it to be a white bowl of a prodigious height and bigness; and when I came up to it I touched it, and found it to be very smooth. I went round to see if it was open on any side, but saw it was not, and that there was no climbing up to the top of it, it was so smooth. It was at least fifty paces round.

By this time the sun was ready to set, and all of a sudden the sky became as dark as if it had been covered with a thick cloud. I was much astonished at this sudden darkness, but much more when I found it was occasioned by a bird, of a monstrous size, that came flying towards me. I remembered a fowl, called *roc*, that

I had often heard mariners speak of, and conceived that the great bowl, which I so much admired, must needs be its egg. In short, the bird lighted, and sat over the egg to hatch it. As I perceived her coming, I crept close to the egg, so that I had before me one of the legs of the bird, which was as big as the trunk of a tree. I tied myself strongly to it with the cloth that went round my turban, in hopes that when the roc flew away next morning she would carry me with her out of this desert island. And after having passed the night in this condition, the bird really flew away next morning, as soon as it was day, and carried me so high that I could not see the earth. Then she descended all of a sudden, with so much rapidity that I lost my senses; but when the roc was settled, and I found myself upon the ground, I speedily untied the knot, and had scarcely done so when the bird, having taken up a serpent of a monstrous length in her bill, flew away.

The place where she left me was a very deep valley, encompassed on all sides with mountains, so high that they seemed to reach above the clouds, and so full of steep rocks that there was no possibility of getting out of the valley. This was a new perplexity, so that when I compared this place with the desert island from which the roc brought me, I found that I had gained nothing by the change.

As I walked through this valley I perceived it was strewn with diamonds, some of which were of surprising bigness. I took a great deal of pleasure in looking at them; but speedily I saw at a distance such objects as very much diminished my satisfaction, and which I could not look upon without terror; they were a great number of serpents, so big and so long that the least of them was

119

capable of swallowing an elephant. They retired in the day-time to their dens, where they hid themselves from the roc, their enemy, and did not come out but in the night-time.

I spent the day in walking about the valley, resting myself at times in such places as I thought most suitable. When night came on I went into a cave, where I thought I might be in safety. I stopped the mouth of it, which was low and straight, with a great stone, to preserve me from the serpents, but not so exactly fitted as to hinder light from coming in. I supped on part of my provisions, but the serpents, which began to appear, hissing about in the meantime, put me into such extreme fear that you may easily imagine I did not sleep. When day appeared the serpents retired, and I came out of the cave trembling. I can justly say that I walked a long time upon diamonds without feeling an inclination to touch any of them. At last I sat down, and notwithstanding my uneasiness, not having shut my eyes during the night, I fell asleep, after having eaten a little more of my provisions; but I had scarcely shut my eyes, when something that fell by me with great noise awakened me. This was a great piece of fresh meat, and at the same time I saw several others fall down from the rocks in different places.

I had always looked upon it as a fable when I heard mariners and others discourse of the valley of diamonds, and of the stratagems made use of by some merchants to get jewels from thence; but now I found it to be true. For, in reality, those merchants come to the neighbourhood of this valley when the eagles have young ones, and throwing great joints of meat into the valley, the diamonds, upon whose points they fall, stick to them; the eagles, which are stronger in this country than anywhere else, pounce with great force upon those pieces of meat, and carry them to their nests upon the top of the rocks to feed their young with, at which time the merchants, running to their nests, frighten the eagles by their noise, and take away the diamonds that stick to the meat. And this stratagem they make use of to get the diamonds out of the valley, which is surrounded with such precipices that nobody can enter it.

I believed till then that it was not possible for me to get out of this abyss, which I looked upon as my grave; but now I changed my mind, for the falling in of those pieces of meat put me in hopes of a way of saving my life.

I began to gather together the largest diamonds that I could see, and put them into the leathern bag in which I used to carry my provisions. I afterwards took the largest piece of meat I could find, tied it close round me with the cloth of my turban, and then laid myself upon the ground, with my face downwards, the bag of diamonds being tied fast to my girdle, so that it could not possibly drop off.

I had scarcely laid me down before the eagles came. Each of them seized a piece of meat, and one of the strongest having taken me up, with a piece of meat on my back, carried me to his nest on the top of the mountain. The merchants fell straightway to shouting, to frighten the eagles; and when they had obliged them to quit their prey, one of them came to the nest where I was. He was very much afraid when he saw me, but recovering himself, instead of inquiring how I came thither, he began to quarrel with me, and asked why I stole his goods. "You will treat me," replied I, "with more civility when you know me better. Do not trouble yourself; I have diamonds enough for you and myself too, more than all the other merchants together. If they have any, it is by chance; but I chose myself in the bottom of the valley all those which you see in this bag"; and having spoken those words, I showed them to him. I had scarcely done speaking, when the other merchants came trooping about us, much astonished to see me; but they were much more surprised when I told them my story. Yet they did not so much admire my stratagem to save myself as my courage to attempt it.

They took me to the place where they were staying all together, and there having opened my bag, they were surprised at the largeness of my diamonds, and confessed that in all the courts where they had been they had never seen any that came near them. I prayed the merchant to whom the nest belonged (for every merchant had his own), to take as many for his share as he pleased. He contented himself with one, and that too the least of them; and when I pressed him to take more, without fear of doing me any injury, "No," said he, "I am very well satisfied with this, which is valuable enough to save me the trouble of making any more voyages to raise as great a fortune as I desire."

I spent the night with those merchants, to whom I told my story a second time, for the satisfaction of those who had not heard it. I could not moderate my joy when I found myself delivered from the danger I have mentioned. I thought I was in a dream, and could scarcely believe myself to be out of danger.

The merchants had thrown their pieces of meat into the valley for several days, and each of them being satisfied with the diamonds that had fallen to his lot, we left the place next morning all together, and travelled near high mountains, where there were serpents of a prodigous length, which we had the good fortune to escape. We took ship at the nearest port and came to the Isle of Roha, where the trees grow that yield camphor. This tree is so large, and its branches so thick, that a hundred men may easily sit under its shade. The juice of which the camphor is made runs out from a hole bored in the upper part of the tree, is received in a vessel, where it grows thick, and becomes what we call camphor; and the juice thus drawn out the tree withers and dies.

There is in this island the rhinoceros, a creature less than the elephant, but greater than the buffalo; it has a horn upon its nose about a cubit long; this horn is solid, and cleft in the middle from one end to the other, and there are upon it white lines, representing the figure of a man. The rhinoceros fights with the elephant, runs his horn into him, and carries him off upon his head; but the blood of the elephant running into his eyes and making him blind, he falls to the ground, and then, strange to relate, the roc comes and carries them both away in her claws to be food for her young ones.

Here I exchanged some of my diamonds for good merchandise. From thence we went to other isles, and at last, having touched at several trading towns of the main land, we landed at Balsora, from whence I went to Bagdad. There I immediately gave great alms to the poor, and lived honourably upon the vast riches I had gained with so much fatigue.

THE THIRD VOYAGE OF
SINBAD THE SAILOR

The pleasures of the life which I then led soon made me forget the risks I had run in my two former voyages; but, being then in the flower of my age, I grew weary of living without business; and hardening myself against the thought of any danger I might incur, I went from Bagdad, with the richest commodities of the country, to Balsora: there I embarked again with the merchants. We made a long voyage, and touched at several ports, where we drove a considerable trade. One day, being out in the main ocean, we were attacked by a horrible tempest, which made us lose our course. The tempest continued several days, and brought us before the port of an island, where the captain was very unwilling to enter; but we were obliged to cast anchor there. When we had furled our sails the captain told us that this and some other neighbouring islands were inhabited by hairy savages, who would speedily attack us; and though they were but dwarfs, yet our misfortune was that we must make no resistance, for they were more in number than the locusts; and if we happened to kill one of them they would all fall upon us and destroy us.

This discourse of the captain put the whole company into a great consternation; and we found very soon, to our cost, that what he had told us was but too true; an innumerable multitude of frightful savages, covered all over with red hair, and about two feet high, came swimming towards us, and in a little time encompassed our ship. They spoke to us as they came near, but we understood not their language; they climbed up the sides of the ship with an agility that surprised us. We beheld all this with mortal fear, without daring to offer to defend ourselves, or to speak one word to divert them from their mischievous design. In short, they took down our sails, cut the cable, and, hauling to the shore, made us all get out, and afterwards carried the ship into another island, from whence they had come. All travellers carefully avoided that island where they left us, it being very dangerous to stay there, for a reason you shall hear anon; but we were forced to bear our affliction with patience.

We went forward into the island, where we found some fruits and herbs to prolong our lives as long as we could; but we expected nothing but death. As we went on we perceived at a distance a great pile of building, and made towards it. We found it to be a palace, well built, and very lofty, with a gate of ebony with double doors, which we thrust open. We entered the court, where we saw before us a vast apartment with a porch, having on one side a heap of men's bones, and on the other a vast number of roasting spits. We trembled at this spectacle, and, being weary with travelling, our legs failed under us: we fell to the ground, seized with deadly fear, and lay a long time motionless.

The sun had set, and whilst we were in the lamentable condition just mentioned, the gate of the apartment opened with a great noise, and there came out the horrible figure of a black man, as high as a tall palm tree. He had but one eye, and that in the middle of his forehead, where it looked as red as a burning coal. His fore-teeth were very long and sharp, and stood out of his mouth, which was as deep as that of a horse; his upper lip hung down upon his breast; his ears resembled those of an elephant, and covered his shoulders; and his nails were as long and crooked as the talons of the greatest birds. At the sight of so frightful a giant we lost all our senses, and lay like men dead.

At last we came to ourselves, and saw him sitting in the porch, looking at us. When he had considered us well, he advanced towards us, and laying his hand upon me, he took me up by the nape of my neck, and turned me round as a butcher would do a sheep's head. After having viewed me well, and perceiving me to be so lean that I had nothing but skin and bone, he let me go. He took up all the rest, one by one, and viewed them in the same manner; and the captain being the fattest, he held him with one hand, as I might a sparrow, and thrusting a spit through him, kindled a great fire, roasted, and ate him in his apartment for his supper. This being done, he returned to his porch, where he lay and fell asleep, snoring louder than thunder. He slept thus till morning. For our parts, it was not possible for us to enjoy any rest; so that we passed the night in the most cruel fear that can be imagined. Day being come, the giant awoke, got up, went out, and left us in the palace.

When we thought him at a distance, we broke the melancholy silence we had kept all night, and every one grieving more than another, we made the palace

126

resound with our complaints and groans. Though there were a great many of us, and we had but one enemy, we had not at first the presence of mind to think of delivering ourselves from him by his death.

We thought of several other things, but determined nothing; so that, submitting to what it should please God to order concerning us, we spent the day in running about the island for fruit and herbs to sustain our lives. When evening came, we sought for a place to lie down in, but found none; so that we were forced, whether we would or not, to return to the palace.

The giant failed not to come back, and supped once more upon one of our companions; after which he slept, and snored till day, and then went out and left us as formerly. Our condition was so very terrible that several of my comrades designed to throw themselves into the sea, rather than die so strange a death. Those who were of this mind argued with the rest to follow their example; upon which one of the company answered that we were forbidden to destroy ourselves; but even if it were lawful, it was more reasonable to think of a way to rid ourselves of the barbarous tyrant who designed so cruel a death for us.

Having thought of a project for that end, I communicated the same to my comrades, who approved it. "Brethren," said I, "you know there is a great deal of timber floating upon the coast; if you will be advised by me, let us make several rafts that may carry us, and when they are done, leave them there till we think fit to make use of them. In the meantime we will execute the design to deliver ourselves from the giant, and if it succeed, we may stay here with patience till some ship pass by to carry us out of this fatal island; but if it happen to miscarry, we will speedily get to our rafts, and put to sea. I confess, that by exposing ourselves to the fury of the waves, we run a risk of losing our lives; but if we do, is it not better to be buried in the sea than in the entrails of this monster, who has already devoured two of us?" My advice was relished, and we made rafts capable of carrying three persons each.

We returned to the palace towards evening, and the giant arrived a little while after. We were forced to see another of our comrades roasted. But at last we revenged ourselves on the brutish giant thus. After he had made an end of his cursed supper, he lay down on his back, and fell asleep. As soon as we heard him snore, according to his custom, nine of the boldest among us, and myself, took each of us a spit, and putting the points of them into the fire till they were burning hot, we thrust them into his eye all at once, and blinded him. The pain occasioned him to make a frightful cry, and to get up and stretch out his hands in order to sacrifice some of us to his rage, but we ran to places where he could not find us; and after having sought for us in vain, he groped for the gate, and went out, howling dreadfully.

We went out of the palace after the giant, and came to the shore, where we had left our rafts, and put them immediately into the sea. We waited till day in order to get upon them, in case the giant came towards us with any guide of his own species; but we hoped that if he did not appear by sunrise, and gave over his howling, which we still heard, he would die; and if that happened to be the case, we resolved to stay in the island, and not to risk our lives upon the rafts. But day had scarcely appeared when we perceived our cruel enemy, accompanied by two others almost of the same size leading him, and a great number more coming before him with a very quick pace.

When we saw this, we made no delay, but got immediately upon our rafts, and rowed off from the shore. The giants, who perceived this, took up great stones, and running to the shore entered the water up to their waists, and threw so exactly that they sank all the rafts but that I was upon, and all my companions, except the two with me, were drowned. We rowed with all our might, and got out of the reach of the giants; but when we got out to sea, we were exposed to the mercy of the waves and winds, and tossed about, sometimes on one side, and sometimes on another, and spent that night and the following day under a cruel uncertainty as to our fate; but next morning we had the good luck to be thrown upon an island, where we landed with much joy. We found excellent fruit there, that gave us great relief, so that we pretty well recovered our strength.

In the evening we fell asleep on the bank of the sea, but were awakened by the noise of a serpent as long as a palm tree, whose scales made a rustling as he crept along. He swallowed up one of my comrades, notwithstanding his loud cries and the efforts he made to rid himself from the serpent, which shook him several times against the ground, and crushed him; and we could hear him gnaw and tear the poor wretch's bones, when we had fled a great distance from him. Next day we saw the serpent again, to our great terror, and I cried out, "O heaven, to what dangers are we exposed! We rejoiced yesterday at having escaped from the cruelty of a giant and the rage of the waves, and now are we fallen into another danger altogether as terrible."

As we walked about we saw a large tall tree, upon which we designed to pass the following night, for our security; and having satisfied our hunger with fruit, we mounted it accordingly. A little while after, the serpent came hissing to the root of the tree, raised itself up against the trunk of it, and meeting with my comrade, who sat lower than I, swallowed him at once, and went off.

I staid upon the tree till it was day, and then came down, more like a dead man than one alive, expecting the same fate as my two companions. This filled me with horror, so that I was going to throw myself into the sea; but nature prompting us to a desire to live as long as we can, I withstood this temptation to despair, and submitted myself to the will of God, who disposes of our lives at His pleasure.

In the meantime I gathered together a great quantity of small wood, brambles, and dry thorns, and making them up into faggots made a great circle with them round the tree, and also tied some of them to the branches over my head. Having done thus, when the evening came I shut myself up within this circle, with this melancholy piece of satisfaction, that I had neglected nothing which could preserve me from the cruel destiny with which I was threatened. The serpent failed not to come at the usual hour, and went round the tree, seeking for an opportunity to devour me, but was prevented by the rampart I had made, so that he lay till day, like a cat

130

watching in vain for a mouse that has retreated to a place of safety. When day appeared he retired, but I dared not to leave my fort until the sun arose.

I was fatigued with the toil he had put me to, and suffered so much from his poisonous breath that, death seeming preferable to me than the horror of such a condition, I came down from the tree, and not thinking on the resignation I had made to the will of God the preceding day, I ran towards the sea, with a design to throw myself into it headlong.

God took compassion on my desperate state, for just as I was going to throw myself into the sea, I perceived a ship at a considerable distance. I called as loud as I could, and taking the linen from my turban, displayed it that they might observe me. This had the desired effect; all the crew perceived me, and the captain sent his boat for me. As soon as I came aboard, the merchants and seamen flocked about me to know how I came to that desert island; and after I had told them of all that befell me, the oldest among them said they had several times heard of the giants that dwelt in that island, that they were cannibals and ate men raw as well as roasted; and as to the serpents, he added, there were abundance in the isle that hid themselves by day and came abroad by night. After having testified their joy at my escaping so many dangers, they brought me the best of what they had to eat; and the captain, seeing that I was all in rags, was so generous as to give me one of his own suits.

We were at sea for some time, touched at several islands, and at last landed at that of Salabat, where there grows sanders, a wood of great use in physic. We entered the port, and came to anchor. The merchants began to unload their goods, in order to sell or exchange them. In the meantime the captain came to me, and said, "Brother, I have here a parcel of goods that belonged to a merchant who sailed some time on board this ship; and he being dead, I intend to dispose of them for the benefit of his heirs, when I know them." The bales he spoke of lay on the deck, and showing them to me, he said, "There are the goods; I hope you will take care to sell them, and you shall have a commission." I thanked him that he gave me an opportunity to employ myself, because I hated to be idle.

The clerk of the ship took an account of all the bales, with the names of the merchants to whom they belonged; and when he asked the captain in whose name he should enter those he gave me the charge of, "Enter them" said the captain, "in the name of Sinbad the sailor." I could not hear myself named without some emotion, and looking steadfastly on the captain, I knew him to be the person who, in my second voyage, had left me in the island where I fell asleep by a brook, and set sail without me, and without sending to look for me. But I could not remember him at first, he was so much altered since I saw him.

And as for him, who believed me to be dead, I could not wonder at his not knowing me. "But, captain," said I, "was the merchant's name to whom those goods belonged Sinbad?"

"Yes," replied he, "that was his name; he came from Bagdad, and embarked on board my ship at Balsora. One day, when we landed at an island to take in water and other refreshments, I know not by what mistake I set sail without observing that he did not re-embark with us; neither I nor the merchants perceived it till four hours after. We had the wind in our stern and so fresh a gale that it was not then possible for us to tack about for him."

"You believe him then to be dead?" said I.

"Certainly," answered he.

"No, captain," said I; "look upon me, and you may know that I am Sinbad, whom you left in that desert island. I fell asleep by a brook, and when I awoke I found all the company gone."

The captain, having considered me attentively, knew me at last, embraced me, and said, "God be praised that fortune has supplied my defect. There are your goods, which I always took care to preserve and to make the best of at every port where I touched. I restore them to you, with the profit I have made on them." I took them from him, and at the same time acknowledged how much I owed to him.

From the Isle of Salabat we went to another, where I furnished myself with cloves, cinnamon, and other spices. As we sailed from that island we saw a tortoise that was twenty cubits in length and breadth. We observed also a fish which looked like a cow, and gave milk, and its skin is so hard that they usually make bucklers of it. I saw another which had the shape and colour of a camel. In short, after a long voyage, I arrived at Balsora, and from thence returned to this city of Bagdad, with so much riches that I knew not what I had. I gave a great deal to the poor, and bought another great estate in addition to what I had already.

THE FOURTH VOYAGE OF
SINBAD THE SAILOR

The pleasures I took after my third voyage had not
charms enough to divert me from another. I was again
prevailed upon by my passion for traffic and curiosity
to see new things. I therefore settled my affairs, and
having provided a stock of goods fit for the places
where I designed to trade, I set out on my journey.
I took the way of Persia, of which I travelled over
several provinces, and then arrived at a port, where I
embarked. We set sail, and having touched at several
ports of the mainland and some of the eastern islands,
we put out to sea, and were overtaken by a sudden
gust of wind that obliged the captain to furl his sails,
and to take all other necessary precautions to prevent
the danger that threatened us. But all was in vain; our
endeavours had no effect, the sails were torn into a
thousand pieces, and the ship was stranded; so that a
great many of the merchants and seamen were drowned,
and the cargo lost.

I had the good fortune, with several of the merchants
and mariners, to get a plank, and we were carried by
the current to an island which lay before us: there we
found fruit and spring water, which preserved our lives.
We stayed all night near the place where the sea cast

us ashore, without consulting what we should do, our misfortune had dispirited us so much.

Next morning, as soon as the sun was up, we walked from the shore, and advancing into the island, saw some houses, to which we went; and as soon as we came thither we were encompassed by a great number of black men, who seized us, shared us among them, and carried us to their respective habitations.

I and five of my comrades were carried to one place; they made us sit down immediately, and gave us a certain herb, which they made signs to us to eat. My comrades, not taking notice that the black men ate none of it themselves, consulted only the satisfying of their own hunger, and fell to eating with greediness: but I, suspecting some trick, would not so much as taste it, which happened well for me; for in a little time I perceived my companions had lost their senses, and that when they spoke to me they knew not what they said.

The black men fed us afterwards with rice, prepared with oil of cocoanuts, and my comrades, who had lost their reason, ate of it greedily. I ate of it also, but very sparingly. The black men gave us that herb at first on purpose to deprive us of our senses, that we might not be aware of the sad destiny prepared for us; and they gave us rice on purpose to fatten us, for, being cannibals, their design was to eat us as soon as we grew fat. They did accordingly eat my comrades, who were not aware of their condition; but my senses being entire, you may easily guess that instead of growing fat, as the rest did, I grew leaner every day. The fear of death under which I laboured turned all my food into poison. I fell into a languishing illness which proved my safety, for the black men having killed and eaten up my companions, seeing me to be withered, lean, and sick, deferred my death till another time.

Meanwhile, I had a great deal of liberty, so that there was scarcely any notice taken of what I did, and this gave me an opportunity one day to get at a distance from the houses, and to make my escape. An old man who saw me, and suspected my design, called to me as loud as he could to return, but instead of obeying him, I redoubled my pace, and quickly got out of sight. At that time there was none but the old man about the houses, the rest being away, and not to come home till night, which was pretty usual with them; therefore, being sure that they could not come in time to pursue me, I went on till night, when I stopped to rest a little, and to eat some of the provisions I had taken care to bring; but I speedily set forward again, and travelled seven days, avoiding those places which seemed to be inhabited, and living for the most part upon cocoanuts, which served me for both meat and drink. On the eighth day I came near the sea, and all of a sudden saw white people like myself, gathering pepper, of which there was great plenty in that place. This I took to be a good omen, and went to them without any scruple.

The people who gathered pepper came to meet me as soon as they saw me, and asked me in Arabic who I was, and whence I came. I was overjoyed to hear them speak in my own language, and satisfied their curiosity by giving them an account of my shipwreck, and how I fell into the hands of the black men. "Those black men," replied they, "are cannibals, and by what miracle did you escape their cruelty?" I told them the same story I now tell you, at which they were wonderfully surprised.

I stayed with them till they had gathered their quantity of pepper, and then sailed with them to the island from whence they came. They presented me to their king, who was a good prince. He had the patience to hear the relation of my adventures, which surprised him, and he afterwards gave me clothes, and commanded care to be taken of me.

The island was very well peopled, plentiful in everything, and the capital was a place of great trade. This agreeable retreat was very comfortable to me after my misfortune, and the kindness of this generous prince towards me completed my satisfaction. In a word, there was not a person more in favour with him than myself; and, in consequence, every man in court and city sought to oblige me, so that in a very little time I was looked upon rather as a native than a stranger.

I observed one thing which to me appeared very extraordinary. All the people, the king himself not excepted, rode their horses without bridle or stirrups. This made me one day take the liberty to ask the king how that came to pass. His majesty answered, that I talked to him of things which nobody knew the use of in his dominions. I went immediately to a workman, and gave him a model for making the stock of a saddle. When that was done, I covered it myself with velvet and leather, and embroidered it with gold. I afterwards went to a locksmith, who made me a bridle according to the pattern I showed him, and then he made me also some stirrups. When I had all things completed, I presented them to the king, and put them upon one of his horses. His majesty mounted immediately, and was so pleased with them, that he testified his satisfaction by large presents to me. I could not avoid making several others for his ministers and the principal officers of his household, who all of them made me presents that enriched me in a little time. I also made some for the people of best quality in the city, which gained me great reputation and regard.

As I paid court very constantly to the king, he said to me one day, "Sinbad, I love thee; and all my subjects who know thee treat thee according to my example. I have one thing to demand of thee, which thou must grant."

"Sir," answered I, "there is nothing but I will do, as a mark of my obedience to your majesty, whose power over me is absolute."

"I have a mind thou shouldst marry," replied he, "that so thou mayst stay in my dominion, and think no more of thy own country."

I dared not resist the prince's will, and so he gave me one of the ladies of his court, a noble, beautiful, and rich lady. The ceremonies of marriage being over, I went and dwelt with the lady, and for some time we lived together in perfect harmony. I was not, however, very well satisfied with my condition, and therefore designed to make my escape on the first occasion, and to return to Bagdad, which my present settlement, how advantageous soever, could not make me forget.

While I was thinking on this, the wife of one of my neighbours, with whom I had contracted a very close friendship, fell sick and died. I went to see and comfort him in his affliction, and finding him swallowed up with sorrow, I said to him as soon as I saw him, "God preserve you and grant you a long life."

"Alas!" replied he, "how do you think I should obtain that favour you wish me? I have not above an hour to live."

"Pray," said I, "do not entertain such a melancholy thought; I hope it will not be so, but that I shall enjoy your company for many years."

"I wish you," said he, "a long life; but for me my days are at an end, for I must be buried this day with my wife. This is a law which our ancestors established in this island, and always observed inviolably. The living husband is interred with the dead wife, and the living wife with the dead husband. Nothing can save me; every one must submit to this law."

While he was entertaining me with an account of this barbarous custom, the very hearing of which frightened me cruelly, his kindred, friends and neighbours came in a body to assist at the funerals. They put on the corpse the woman's richest apparel, as if it had been her wedding-day, and dressed her with all her jewels; then they put her into an open coffin, and lifting it up, began their march to the place of burial. The husband walked at the head of the company, and followed the corpse. They went up to a high mountain, and when they came thither, took up a great stone, which covered the mouth of a very deep pit, and let down the corpse, with all its apparel and jewels. Then the husband, embracing his kindred and friends, suffered himself to be put into another open coffin without resistance, with a pot of water, and seven little loaves, and was let down in the same manner as they let down his wife. The mountain was pretty long, and reached to the sea. The ceremony being over, they covered the hole again with the stone, and returned.

It is needless to say that I was the only melancholy spectator of this funeral, whereas the rest were scarcely moved at it, the practice was so customary to them. I could not forbear speaking my thoughts of this matter to the king. "Sir," said I, "I cannot but wonder at the strange custom in this country of burying the living with the dead. I have been a great traveller, and seen many countries, but never heard of so cruel a law."

"What do you mean, Sinbad?" said the king; "it is a common law. I shall be interred with the queen, my wife, if she die first."

"But, sir," said I, "may I presume to ask your majesty if strangers be obliged to observe this law?"

"Without doubt," replied the king, smiling at my question; "they are not exempted, if they are married in this island."

I went home very melancholy at this answer, for the fear of my wife dying first, and my being interred alive with her, occasioned me very mortifying reflections. But there was no remedy: I must have patience, and submit to the will of God. I trembled, however, at every little indisposition of my wife; but alas! in a little time my fears came upon me all at once, for she fell ill, and died in a few days.

You may judge of my sorrow; to be interred alive seemed to me as deplorable an end as to be devoured by cannibals. But I must submit; the king and all his court would honour the funeral with their presence, and the most considerable people of the city would do the like. When all was ready for the ceremony, the corpse was put into a coffin, with all her jewels and magnificent apparel.

The cavalcade began, and, as second actor in this doleful tragedy, I went next to the corpse, with my eyes full of tears, bewailing my deplorable fate. Before I came to the mountain, I addressed myself to the king, in the first place, and then to all those who were round me, and bowing before them to the earth to kiss the border of their garments, I prayed them to have compassion upon me. "Consider," said I, "that I am a stranger, and ought not to be subject to this rigorous law, and that I have another wife and child in my own country." It was to no purpose for me to speak thus, no soul was moved at it; on the contrary, they made haste to let down my wife's corpse into the pit, and put me down the next moment in an open coffin, with a vessel full of water and seven loaves. In short, the fatal ceremony being performed, they covered up the mouth of the pit, notwithstanding the excess of my grief and my lamentable cries.

As I came near the bottom, I discovered, by help of the little light that came from above, the nature of this subterranean place; it was a vast long cave, and might be about fifty fathoms deep. I immediately smelt an insufferable stench proceeding from the multitude of corpses which I saw on the right and left; nay, I fancied that I heard some of them sigh out their last. However, when I got down, I immediately left my coffin, and, getting at a distance from the corpses, lay down upon the ground, where I stayed a long time, bathed in tears. Then reflecting on my sad lot, "It is true," said I, "that God disposes all things according to the decrees of His providence; but, poor Sinbad, art not thou thyself the cause of thy being brought to die so strange a death? Would to God thou hadst perished in some of those tempests which thou hast escaped! Then thy death had not been so lingering and terrible in all its circumstances. But thou hast drawn all this upon thyself by thy cursed avarice. Ah! unfortunate wretch, shouldst thou not rather have stayed at home, and quietly enjoyed the fruits of thy labour?"

Such were the vain complaints with which I made the cave echo, beating my head and breast out of rage and despair, and abandoning myself to the most afflicting thoughts. Nevertheless, I must tell you that, instead of calling death to my assistance in that miserable condition, I felt still an inclination to live, and to do all I could to prolong my days. I went groping about, with my nose stopped, for the bread and water that was in my coffin, and took some of it. Though the darkness of the cave was so great that I could not distinguish day and night, yet I always found my coffin again, and the cave seemed to be more spacious and fuller of corpses than it appeared to me at first. I lived for some days upon my bread and water, which being all used up at last I prepared for death.

As I was thinking of death, I heard something walking, and blowing or panting as it walked. I advanced towards that side from whence I heard the noise, and upon my approach the thing puffed and blew harder, as if it had been running away from me. I followed the noise, and the thing seemed to stop sometimes, but always fled and blew as I approached. I followed it so long and so far that at last I perceived a light

142

resembling a star; I went on towards that light, and sometimes lost sight of it, but always found it again, and at last discovered that it came through a hole in the rock large enough for a man to get out at.

Upon this I stopped some time to rest myself, being much fatigued with pursuing this discovery so fast. Afterwards coming up to the hole I went out at it, and found myself upon the shore of the sea. I leave you to guess the excess of my joy; it was such that I could scarce persuade myself of its being real.

But when I had recovered from my surprise, and was convinced of the truth of the matter, I found that the thing which I had followed and heard puff and blow was a creature which came out of the sea, and was accustomed to enter at that hole to feed upon the dead carcasses.

I examined the mountain, and perceived it to be situated betwixt the sea and the town, but without any passage or way to communicate with the latter, the rocks on the side of the sea were so rugged and steep. I fell down upon the shore to thank God for this mercy, and afterwards entered the cave again to fetch bread and water, which I did by daylight, with a better appetite than I had done since my interment in the dark hole.

I returned thither again, and groped about among the biers for all the diamonds, rubies, pearls, gold bracelets, and rich stuffs I could find. These I brought to the shore, and, tying them up neatly into bales with the cords that let down the coffins, I laid them together upon the bank to wait till some ship passed by, without fear of rain, for it was not then the season.

After two or three days I perceived a ship that had but just come out of the harbour and passed near the place where I was. I made a sign with the linen of my turban, and called to them as loud as I could. They heard me, and sent a boat to bring me on board, when the mariners asked by what misfortune I came thither. I told them that I had suffered shipwreck two days ago, and made shift to get ashore with the goods they saw. It was happy for me that those people did not consider the place where I was, nor inquire into the probability of what I told them; but without any more ado took me on board with my goods. When I came to the ship, the captain was so well pleased to have saved me, and so much taken up with his own affairs, that he also took the story of my pretended shipwreck upon trust, and generously refused some jewels which I offered him.

We passed with a regular wind by several islands, among others the one called the Isle of Bells, about ten days' sail from Serendib, and six from that of Kela, where we landed. This island produces lead from its mines, Indian canes, and excellent camphor.

The king of the Isle of Kela is very rich and potent, and the Isle of Bells, which is about two days' journey in extent, is also subject to him. The inhabitants are so barbarous that they still eat human flesh. After we had finished our commerce in that island we put to sea again, and touched at several other ports. At last I arrived happily at Bagdad with infinite riches of which it is needless to trouble you with the detail. Out of thankfulness to God for His mercies, I gave great alms for the support of several mosques, and for the subsistence of the poor, and employed myself wholly

in enjoying the society of my kindred and friends, and in
making merry with them.

THE FIFTH VOYAGE OF
SINBAD THE SAILOR

The pleasures I enjoyed again had charm enough to
make me forget all the troubles and calamities I had
undergone, without curing me of my inclination to make
new voyages. Therefore I bought goods, ordered them
to be packed up and loaded, and set out with them for
the best seaport; and there, that I might not be obliged
to depend upon a captain, but have a ship at my own
command, I waited till one was built on purpose at
my own expense. When the ship was ready, I went
on board with my goods; but not having enough to
load her, I took on board with me several merchants
of different nations, with their merchandise.

We sailed with the first fair wind, and after a long
voyage, the first place we touched at was a desert
island, where we found an egg of a roc, equal in size
to that I formerly mentioned. There was a young roc
in it just ready to be hatched, and the bill of it began
to appear.

The merchants whom I had taken on board my ship,
and who landed with me, broke the egg with hatchets,
and made a hole in it, from whence they pulled out the

young roc piece by piece, and roasted it. I had earnestly persuaded them not to meddle with the egg, but they would not listen to me.

Scarcely had they made an end of their feast, when there appeared in the air, at a considerable distance from us, two great clouds. The captain whom I hired to manage my ship, knowing by experience what it meant, cried that it was the cock and hen roc that belonged to the young one, and pressed us to re-embark with all speed, to prevent the misfortune which he saw would otherwise befall us. We made haste to do so, and set sail with all possible diligence.

In the meantime the two rocs approached with a frightful noise, which they redoubled when they saw the egg broken, and their young one gone. But having a mind to avenge themselves, they flew back towards the place from whence they came, and disappeared for some time, while we made all the sail we could to prevent that which unhappily befell us.

They returned, and we observed that each of them carried between their talons stones, or rather rocks, of a monstrous size. When they came directly over my ship, they hovered, and one of them let fall a stone; but by the dexterity of the steersman, who turned the ship with the rudder, it missed us, and falling by the side of the ship into the sea, divided the water so that we could see almost to the bottom. The other roc, to our misfortune, threw the stone so exactly upon the middle of the ship that it split into a thousand pieces. The mariners and passengers were all killed by the stone, or sunk. I myself had the last fate; but as I came up again I fortunately caught hold of a piece of the wreck, and swimming sometimes with one hand and sometimes with the other, but always holding fast to my board, the wind and the tide favouring me, I came to an island, where the beach was very steep. I overcame that difficulty however, and got ashore.

I sat down upon the grass, to recover myself a little from my fatigue, after which I got up, and went into the island to view it. It seemed to be a delicious garden. I found trees everywhere, some of them bearing green and others ripe fruits, and streams of fresh pure water, with pleasant windings and turnings. I ate of the fruits, which I found excellent, and drank of the water, which was very pleasant.

Night being come, I lay down upon the grass in a convenient place enough, but I could not sleep for an hour at a time, my mind was so disturbed with the fear of being alone in so desert a place. Thus I spent the best part of the night in fretting, and reproached myself for my imprudence in not staying at home, rather than undertaking this last voyage. These reflections carried me so far, that I began to form a design against my own life, but daylight dispersed these melancholy thoughts, and I got up, and walked among the trees, but not without apprehensions of danger.

When I was a little advanced into the island, I saw an old man who appeared very weak and feeble. He sat upon the bank of a stream, and at first I took him to be one who had been shipwrecked like myself. I went towards him and saluted him, but he only bowed his head a little. I asked him what he did there, but instead of answering he made a sign for me to take him upon

147

my back and carry him over the brook, signifying that it was to gather fruit.

I believed him really to stand in need of my help, so took him upon my back, and having carried him over, bade him get down, and for that end stooped that he might get off with ease: but instead of that (which I laugh at every time I think of it), the old man, who to me had appeared very decrepit, clasped his legs nimbly about my neck, and then I perceived his skin to resemble that of a cow. He sat astride upon my shoulders, and held my throat so tight that I thought he would have strangled me, the fright of which made me faint away and fall down.

Notwithstanding my fainting, the ill-natured old fellow kept fast about my neck, but opened his legs a little to give me time to recover my breath. When I had done so, he thrust one of his feet against my stomach, and struck me so rudely on the side with the other, that he forced me to rise up against my will. Having got up, he made me walk under the trees, and forced me now and then to stop, to gather and eat fruit such as we found. He never left me all day, and when I lay down to rest by night, he laid himself down with me, always holding fast about my neck. Every morning he pushed me to make me wake, and afterwards obliged me to get up and walk, and pressed me with his feet. You may judge then what trouble I was in, to be loaded with such a burden as I could by no means rid myself of.

One day I found in my way several dry calabashes that had fallen from a tree; I took a large one, and, after cleaning it, pressed into it some juice of grapes, which abounded in the island. Having filled the calabash, I set

148

it in a convenient place; and coming hither again some days after, I took up my calabash, and setting it to my mouth found the wine to be so good that it presently made me not only forget my sorrow, but grow vigorous, and so light-hearted that I began to sing and dance as I walked along.

The old man, perceiving the effect which this drink had upon me, and that I carried him with more ease than I did before, made a sign for me to give him some of it. I gave him the calabash, and the liquor pleasing his palate, he drank it all off. He became drunk immediately, and the fumes getting up into his head he began to sing after his manner, and to dance upon my shoulders. His jolting about made him sick, and he loosened his legs from about me by degrees; so finding that he did not press me as before, I threw him upon the ground, where he lay without motion, and then I took up a great stone, with which I crushed his head to pieces.

I was extremely rejoiced to be freed thus for ever from this cursed old fellow, and walked along the shore of the sea, where I met the crew of a ship that had cast anchor to take in water to refresh themselves. They were extremely surprised to see me, and to hear the particulars of my adventures. "You fell," said they, "into the hands of the old man of the sea, and are the first that has ever escaped strangling by him. He never left those he had once made himself master of till he destroyed them, and he has made this island famous for the number of men he has slain; so that the merchants and mariners who landed upon it dared not advance into the island but in numbers together."

After having informed me of these things they carried

me with them to the ship; the captain received me with great satisfaction when they told him what had befallen me. He put out again to sea, and after some days' sail we arrived at the harbour of a great city, where the houses were built of good stone.

One of the merchants of the ship, who had taken me into his friendship, asked me to go along with him, and took me to a place appointed as a retreat for foreign merchants. He gave me a great bag, and having recommended me to some people of the town, who were used to gather cocoanuts, he desired them to take me with them to do the like: "Go," said he, "follow them, and do as you see them do, and do not separate from them, otherwise you endanger your life." Having thus spoken, he gave me provisions for the journey, and I went with them.

We came to a great forest of trees, extremely straight and tall, their trunks so smooth that it was not possible for any man to climb up to the branches that bore the fruit. All the trees were cocoanut trees, and when we entered the forest we saw a great number of apes of all sizes, that fled as soon as they perceived us, and climbed up to the top of the trees with surprising swiftness.

The merchants with whom I was gathered stones, and threw them at the apes on the top of the trees. I did the same, and the apes, out of revenge, threw cocoanuts at us as fast and with such gestures as sufficiently testified their anger and resentment: we gathered up the cocoanuts, and from time to time threw stones to provoke the apes: so that by this stratagem we filled our bags with cocoanuts, which it had been impossible for us to do otherwise.

When we had gathered our number, we returned to the city, where the merchant who sent me to the forest gave me the value of the cocoanuts I had brought; "Go on," said he, "and do the like every day, until you have money enough to carry you home." I thanked him for his good advice, and gathered together as many cocoanuts as amounted to a considerable sum.

The vessel in which I came sailed with merchants who loaded her with cocoanuts. I expected the arrival of another, whose merchants landed speedily for the like loading. I embarked on board the same all the cocoanuts that belonged to me, and when she was ready to sail I went and took leave of the merchant who had been so kind to me; but he could not embark with me because he had not finished his business.

We set sail towards the islands where pepper grows in great plenty. From thence we went to the Isle of Comari, where the best sort of wood of aloes grows, and whose inhabitants have made it an inviolable law to drink no wine themselves, nor to suffer any kind of improper conduct. I exchanged my cocoanuts in those two islands for pepper and wood of aloes, and went with other merchants pearl-fishing. I hired divers, who fetched me up those that were very large and pure. Then I embarked joyfully in a vessel that happily arrived at Balsora; from thence I returned to Bagdad, where I made vast sums by my pepper, wood aloes, and pearls. I gave the tenth of my gains in alms, as I had done upon my return from other voyages, and endeavoured to ease myself from my fatigue by diversions of all sorts.

THE SIXTH VOYAGE OF
SINBAD THE SAILOR

After being shipwrecked five times, and escaping so many dangers, could I resolve again to try my fortune, and expose myself to new hardships? I am astonished at it myself when I think of it, and must certainly have been induced to it by my stars. But be that as it will, after a year's rest I prepared for a sixth voyage, notwithstanding the entreaties of my kindred and friends, who did all that was possible to prevent me. Instead of taking my way by the Persian Gulf, I travelled once more through several provinces of Persia and the Indies, and arrived at a sea-port, where I embarked on board a ship, the captain of which was resolved on a long voyage.

It was very long indeed, but at the same time so unfortunate that the captain and pilot lost their course, and knew not where they were. They found it at last, but we had no reason to rejoice at it. We were all seized with extraordinary fear when we saw the captain quit his post, and cry out. He threw off his turban, pulled his beard, and beat his head like a madman. We asked him the reason, and he answered that he was in the most dangerous place in all the sea. "A rapid current carries the ship along with it," he said, "and we shall all of us perish in less than a quarter of an hour. Pray to God to deliver us from this danger; we cannot escape it if He does not take pity on us." At these words he ordered the sails to be changed; but all the ropes broke, and the ship, without its being possible to help it, was carried by the current to the foot of an inaccessible mountain, where she ran ashore, and was broken to pieces, yet so that we saved our lives, our provisions, and the best of our goods.

This being over, the captain said to us, "God has done what pleased Him; we may every man dig our grave here, and bid the world adieu, for we are all in so fatal a place that none shipwrecked here have ever returned to their homes again." His discourse afflicted us sorely, and we embraced each other with tears in our eyes, bewailing our deplorable lot.

The mountain at the foot of which we were cast was the coast of a very long and large island. This coast was covered all over with wrecks, and from the vast number of men's bones we saw everywhere, and which filled us with horror, we concluded that abundance of people had died there. It is also impossible to tell what a quantity of goods and riches we found cast ashore there. All these objects served only to augment our grief. Whereas in all other places rivers places rivers run from their channels into the sea, here a great river of fresh water runs out of the sea into a dark cave, whose entrance is very high and large. What is most remarkable in this place is that the stones of the mountain are of crystal, rubies, or other precious stones. Here is also a sort of fountain of pitch or bitumen, that runs into the sea, which the fishes swallow, and then vomit up again, turned into ambergris; and this the waves throw up on the beach in great quantities. Here also grow trees, most of which are wood of aloes, equal in goodness to those of Comari.

To finish the description of this place, which may well be called a gulf, since nothing ever returns from it—it is not possible for ships to get away again when once they come near it. If they are driven thither by a wind from the sea, the wind and the current ruin them; and if they come into it when a land-wind blows, which might seem to favour their getting out again, the height of the mountain stops the wind, and occasions a calm, so that the force of the current runs them ashore, where they are broken to pieces, as ours was; and that which completes the misfortune is that there is no possibility to get to the top of the mountain, or to get out any manner of way.

We continued upon the shore, like men out of their senses, and expected death every day. At first we divided our provisions as equally as we could, and thus everyone lived a longer or shorter time, according to their temperance, and the use they made of their provisions.

Those who died first were interred by the rest; and, for my part, I paid the last duty to all my companions. Nor are you to wonder at this; for besides that I husbanded the provision that fell to my share better than they, I had provision of my own, which I did not share with my comrades; yet when I buried the last, I had so little remaining that I thought I could not hold out long: so I dug a grave, resolving to lie down in it, because there was none left to inter me. I must confess to you at the same time that while I was thus employed I could not but reflect upon myself as the cause of my own ruin, and repented that I had ever undertaken this last voyage; nor did I stop at reflections only, but had well nigh hastened my own death, and began to tear my hands with my teeth.

But it pleased God once more to take compassion on me, and put it in my mind to go to the bank of the river which ran into the great cave; where, considering the river with great attention, I said to myself, "This river, which runs thus under ground, must come out somewhere or other. If I make a raft, and leave myself to the current, it will bring me to some inhabited country, or drown me. If I be drowned I lose nothing, but only change one kind of death for another; and if I get out of this fatal place, I shall not only avoid the sad fate of my comrades, but perhaps find some new occasion of enriching myself. Who knows but fortune waits, upon my getting off this dangerous shelf, to compensate my shipwreck with interest?"

I immediately went to work on a raft. I made it of large pieces of timber and cables, for I had choice of them, and tied them together so strongly that I had made a very solid little raft. When I had finished it I loaded it with some bales of rubies, emeralds, ambergris, rock-crystal, and rich stuffs. Having balanced all my cargo exactly and fastened it well to the raft, I went on board it with two little oars that I had made, and, leaving it to the course of the river, I resigned myself to the will of God.

As soon as I came into the cave I lost all light, and the stream carried me I knew not whither. Thus I floated for some days in perfect darkness, and once found the arch so low that it well nigh broke my head, which made me very cautious afterwards to avoid the like danger. All this while I ate nothing but what was just necessary to support nature; yet, notwithstanding this frugality, all my provisions were spent. Then a pleasing sleep fell upon me. I cannot tell how long it continued; but when I awoke, I was surprised to find myself in the middle of a vast country, at the bank of a river, where my raft was tied, amidst a great number of negroes. I got up as soon as I saw them and saluted them. They spoke to me, but I did not understand their language. I was so transported with joy that I knew not whether I was asleep or awake; but being persuaded that I was not asleep, I recited the following words in Arabic aloud: "Call upon the Almighty, he will help thee; thou needest not perplex thyself about anything else; shut thy eyes, and while thou art asleep, God will change thy bad fortune into good."

One of the blacks, who understood Arabic, hearing me speak thus, came towards me and said, "Brother, be not surprised to see us; we are inhabitants of this country, and came hither to-day to water our fields, by digging little canals from this river, which comes out of the neighbouring mountain. We saw something floating upon the water, went speedily to find out what it was, and perceiving your raft, one of us swam into the river, and brought it hither, where we fastened it, as you see, until you should awake. Pray tell us your history, for it must be extraordinary; how did you venture into this river, and whence did you come?"

I begged of them first to give me something to eat, and then I would satisfy their curiosity. They gave me several sorts of food; and when I had satisfied my hunger, I gave them a true account of all that had befallen me, which they listened to with wonder. As soon as I had finished my discourse, they told me, by the person who spoke Arabic and interpreted to them what I said, that it was one of the most surprising stories they ever heard, and that I must go along with them, and tell it to their king myself; the story was too extraordinary to be told by any other than the person to whom it happened. I told them I was ready to do whatever they pleased.

They immediately sent for a horse, which was brought in a little time; and having made me get upon him, some of them walked before me to show me the way, and the rest took my raft and cargo, and followed me.

We marched thus altogether, till we came to the city of Serendib, for it was in that island I landed. The blacks presented me to their king; I approached his throne, and saluted him as I used to do the kings of the Indies, that is to say, I prostrated myself at his feet, and kissed the earth. The prince ordered me to rise up, received me with an obliging air, and made me come up, and sit down near him. He first asked me my name, and I answered, "They call me Sinbad the sailor, because of the many voyages I have undertaken, and I am a citizen of Bagdad."

"But," replied he, "how came you into my dominions, and from whence came you last?"

I concealed nothing from the king; I told him all that I have now told you, and his majesty was so surprised and charmed with it, that he commanded my adventure to be written in letters of gold, and laid up in the archives of his kingdom. At last my raft was brought in, and the bales opened in his presence: he admired the quantity of wood of aloes and ambergris; but, above all, the rubies and emeralds, for he had none in his treasury that came near them.

Observing that he looked on my jewels with pleasure, and viewed the most remarkable among them one after another, I fell prostrate at his feet, and took the liberty to say to him, "Sir, not only my person is at your majesty's service, but the cargo of the raft, and I would beg of you to dispose of it as your own."

He answered me with a smile, "Sinbad, I will take care not to covet anything of yours, nor to take anything from you that God has given you; far from lessening your wealth, I design to augment it, and will not let you go out of my dominions without marks of my liberality."

All the answer I returned was prayers for the prosperity of this prince, and commendations of his generosity and bounty. He charged one of his officers to take care of me, and ordered people to serve me at his own charge. The officer was very faithful in the execution of his orders, and caused all the goods to be carried to the lodgings provided for me. I went every day at a set hour to pay court to the king, and spent the rest of my time in seeing the city, and what was most worthy of notice.

The Isle of Serendib is situated just under the equinoctial line, so that the days and nights there are always of twelve hours each, and the island is eighty parasangs in length, and as many in breadth.

The capital city stands at the end of a fine valley formed by a mountain in the middle of the island, which is the highest in the world. I made, by way of devotion, a pilgrimage to the place where Adam was confined after his banishment from Paradise, and had the curiosity to go to the top of it.

When I came back to the city, I prayed the king to allow me to return to my country, which he granted me in the most obliging and honourable manner. He would needs force a rich present upon me, and when I went to take my leave of him, he gave me one much more valuable, and at the same time charged me with a letter for the Commander of the Faithful, our sovereign, saying to me, "I pray you give this present from me and this letter to Caliph Haroun Alraschid, and assure him of my friendship." I took the present and letter in a very respectful manner, and promised his majesty punctually to execute the commission with which he was pleased to honour me. Before I embarked, this prince sent for the captain and the merchants who were to go with me, and ordered them to treat me with all possible respect.

The letter from the King of Serendib was written on the skin of a certain animal of great value, because of its being so scarce, and of a yellowish colour. The writing was azure, and the contents as follows:-

"The king of the Indies, before whom march a hundred elephants, who lives in a palace that shines with a hundred thousand rubies, and who has in his treasury twenty thousand crowns enriched with diamonds, to Caliph Haroun Alraschid:

"Though the present we send you be inconsiderable, receive it as a brother and a friend, in consideration of the hearty friendship which we bear to you, and of which we are willing to give you proof. We desire the same part in your friendship, considering that we believe it to be our merit, being of the same dignity with yourself. We conjure you this in the rank of a brother. Farewell."

The present consisted first, of one single ruby made into a cup, about half a foot high, an inch thick, and filled with round pearls. Secondly, the skin of a serpent, whose scales were as large as an ordinary piece of gold, and had the virtue to preserve from sickness those who lay upon it. Thirdly, fifty thousand drachms of the best wood of aloes, with thirty grains of camphor as big as pistachios. And fourthly, a she-slave of ravishing beauty, whose apparel was covered all over with jewels.

The ship set sail, and after a very long and successful voyage, we landed at Balsora; from thence I went to Bagdad, where the first thing I did was to acquit myself of my commission.

I took the King of Serendib's letter, and went to present myself at the gate of the Commander of the Faithful, followed by the beautiful slave and such of my own family as carried the presents. I gave an account of the reason of my coming, and was immediately conducted to the throne of the caliph. I made my reverence, and after a short speech gave him the letter and present. When he had read what the King of Serendib wrote to him, he asked me if that prince were really so rich and potent as he had said in this letter. I prostrated myself a second time, and rising again, "Commander of the Faithful," said I, "I can assure your majesty he doth not exceed the truth on that head: I am witness of it. There is nothing more capable of raising a man's admiration than the magnificence of his palace. When the prince appears in public, he has a throne fixed on the back of an elephant, and marches betwixt two ranks of his ministers, favourites, and other people of his court; before him, upon the same elephant, an officer carries a golden lance in his hand, and behind the throne there is another, who stands upright with a column of gold, on the top of which there is an emerald half a foot long and an inch thick; before him march a guard of a thousand men, clad in cloth of gold and silk, and mounted on elephants richly caparisoned.

"While the king is on his march, the officer who is before him on the same elephant cries from time to time, with a loud voice, 'Behold the great monarch, the potent and redoubtable Sultan of the Indies, whose palace is covered with a hundred thousand rubies, and who possesses twenty thousand crowns of diamonds." After he has pronounced these words, the officer behind the throne cries in his turn, "This monarch so great and so powerful, must die, must die, must die." And the officer in front replies, "Praise be to Him who lives for ever."

"Further, the King of Serendib is so just that there are no judges in his dominions. His people have no need of them. They understand and observe justice of themselves."

The caliph was much pleased with my discourse. "The wisdom of this king," said he, "appears in his letter, and after what you tell me I must confess that his wisdom is worthy of his people, and his people deserve so wise as prince." Having spoken thus he dismissed me, and sent me home with a rich present.

THE SEVENTH AND LAST VOYAGE
OF SINBAD THE SAILOR

Being returned from my sixth voyage, I absolutely laid aside all thoughts of travelling any farther; for, besides that my years now required rest, I was resolved no more to expose myself to such risk as I had run; so that I thought of nothing but to pass the rest of my days in quiet. One day, as I was treating some of my friends, one of my servants came and told me that an officer of the caliph asked for me. I rose from the table, and went to him. "The caliph," said he, "has sent me to tell you that he must speak with you." I followed the officer to the palace, where, being presented to the caliph, I saluted him by prostrating myself at his feet. "Sinbad," said he to me, "I stand in need of you; you must do me the service to carry my answer and present to the King of Serendib. It is but just I should return his civility."

This command of the caliph to me was like a clap of thunder. "Commander of the Faithful," replied I, "I am ready to do whatever your majesty shall think fit to command me; but I beseech you most humbly to consider what I have undergone. I have also made a vow never to go out of Bagdad." Here I took occasion to give him a large and particular account of all my adventures, which he had the patience to hear out.

As soon as I had finished, "I confess," said he, "that the things you tell me are very extraordinary, yet you must for my sake undertake this voyage which I propose to you. You have nothing to do but to go to the Isle of Serendib, and deliver the commission which I give you. After that you are at liberty to return. But you must go; for you know it would be indecent, and not suitable to my dignity, to be indebted to the king of that island." Perceiving that the caliph insisted upon it, I submitted, and told him that I was willing to obey. He was very well pleased at it, and ordered me a thousand sequins for the expense of my journey.

I prepared for my departure in a few days, and as soon as the caliph's letter and present were delivered to me, I went to Balsora, where I embarked, and had a very happy voyage. I arrived at the Isle of Serendib, where I acquainted the king's ministers with my commission, and prayed them to get me speedy audience. They did so, and I was conducted to the palace in an honourable manner, where I saluted the king by prostration, according to custom. That prince knew me immediately, and testified very great joy to see me. "O Sinbad," said he, "you are welcome; I swear to you I have many times thought of you since you went hence; I bless the day upon which we see one another once more." I made my compliment to him, and after having thanked him for his kindness to me, I delivered the caliph's letter and present, which he received with all imaginable satisfaction.

The caliph's present was a complete set of cloth of

gold, valued at one thousand sequins; fifty robes of rich stuff, a hundred others of white cloth, the finest of Cairo, Suez, Cusa, and Alexandria; a royal crimson bed, and a second of another fashion; a vessel of agate broader than deep, an inch thick, and half a foot wide, the bottom of which represented in bas-relief a man with one knee on the ground, who held a bow and an arrow, ready to let fly at a lion. He sent him also a rich table, which, according to tradition, belonged to the great Solomon. The caliph's letter was as follows:

"Greeting in the name of the Sovereign Guide of the Right Way, to the potent and happy Sultan, from Abdallah Haroun Alraschid, whom God hath set in the place of honour, after his ancestors of happy memory:

"We received your letter with joy, and send you this from the council of our port, the garden of superior wits. We hope, when you look upon it, you will find our good intention, and be pleased with it. Farewell."

The King of Serendib was highly pleased that the caliph returned his friendship. A little time after this audience, I solicited leave to depart, and had much difficulty to obtain it. I obtained it, however, at last, and the king, when he dismissed me, made me a very considerable present. I embarked immediately to return to Bagdad, but had not the good fortune to arrive there as I hoped. God ordered it otherwise.

Three or four days after my departure, we were attacked by pirates, who easily seized upon our ship. Some of the crew offered resistance, which cost them their lives. But as for me and the rest, who were not so imprudent, the pirates saved us on purpose to make slaves of us.

We were all stripped, and instead of our own clothes they gave us sorry rags, and carried us into a remote island, where they sold us.

I fell into the hands of a rich merchant, who, as soon as he bought me, carried me to his house, treated me well, and clad me handsomely for a slave. Some days after, not knowing who I was, he asked me if I understood any trade. I answered that I was no mechanic, but a merchant, and that the pirates who sold me had robbed me of all I had.

"But tell me," replied he, "can you shoot with a bow?"

I answered that the bow was one of my exercises in my youth, and I had not yet forgotten it. Then he gave me a bow and arrows, and, taking me behind him upon an elephant, carried me to a vast forest some leagues from the town. We went a great way into the forest, and when he thought fit to stop he bade me alight; then showing me a great tree, "Climb up that tree," said he, "and shoot at the elephants as you see them pass by, for there is a prodigious number of them in this forest, and, if any of them fall, come and give me notice of it." Having spoken thus, he left me victuals, and returned to the town, and I continued upon the tree all night.

I saw no elephant during that time, but next morning, as soon as the sun was up, I saw a great number: I shot several arrows among them, and at last one of the elephants fell; the rest retired immediately, and left me at liberty to go and acquaint my patron with my booty. When I had told him the news, he gave me a good meal, commended my dexterity, and caressed me highly. We afterwards went together to the forest, where we dug a hole for the elephant; my patron intending to return when it was rotten, and to take the teeth, etc., to trade with.

I continued this game for two months, and killed an elephant every day, getting sometimes upon one tree, and sometimes upon another. One morning, as I looked for the elephants, I perceived with an extreme amazement that, instead of passing by me across the forest as usual, they stopped, and came to me with a horrible noise, in such a number that the earth was covered with them, and shook under them. They encompassed the tree where I was with their trunks extended and their eyes all fixed upon me. At this frightful spectacle I remained immoveable, and was so much frightened that my bow and arrows fell out of my hand.

My fears were not in vain; for after tne elephants had stared upon me for some time, one of the largest of them put his trunk round the root of the tree, and pulled so strong that he plucked it up and threw it on the ground; I fell with the tree, and the elephant taking me up with his trunk, laid me on his back, where I sat more like one dead than alive, with my quiver on my shoulder: then he put himself at the head of the rest, who followed him in troops, and carried me to a place where he laid me down on the ground, and retired with all his companions. Conceive, if you can, the condition I was in: I thought myself to be in a dream; at last, after having lain some time, and seeing the elephants gone, I got up, and found I was upon a long and broad hill, covered all over with the bones and teeth of elephants. I confess to you that this furnished me with abundance of reflections. I admired the instinct of those animals; I doubted not but that this was their burying place, and that they carried me thither on purpose to tell me that I should forbear to persecute them, since I did it only for their teeth. I did not stay on the hill, but turned towards the city, and, after having travelled a day and a night, I came to my patron; I met no elephant on my way, which made me think they had retired farther into the forest, to leave me at liberty to come back to the hill without any hindrance.

As soon as my patron saw me: "Ah, poor Sinbad," said he, "I was in great trouble to know what had become of you. I have been at the forest, where I found a tree newly pulled up, and a bow and arrows on the ground, and after having sought for you in vain I despaired of ever seeing you more. Pray tell me what befell you, and by what good hap you are still alive."

I satisfied his curiosity, and going both of us next morning to the hill, he found to his great joy that what I had told him was true. We loaded the elephant upon which we came with as many teeth as he could carry; and when we had returned, "Brother," said my patron—"for I will treat you no more as my slave—after having made such a discovery as will enrich me, God bless you with all happiness and prosperity. I declare before Him that I give you your liberty. I concealed from you what I am now going to tell you.

"The elephants of our forest have every year killed a great many slaves, whom we sent to seek ivory. Notwithstanding all the cautions we could give them, those crafty animals killed them one time or other. God has delivered you from their fury, and has bestowed that favour upon you only. It is a sign that He loves you, and has use for your service in the world. You have procured me incredible gain. We could not have ivory formerly but by exposing the lives of our slaves, and now our whole city is enriched by your means. Do not think I pretend to have rewarded you by giving you your liberty; I will also give you considerable riches. I could engage all our city to contribute towards making your fortune, but I will have the glory of doing it myself."

To this obliging discourse I replied, "Patron, God preserve you. Your giving me my liberty is enough to discharge what you owe me, and I desire no other reward for the service I had the good fortune to do to you and your city, than leave to return to my own country."

"Very well," said he, "the monsoon will in a little time bring ships for ivory. I will send you home then, and give you wherewith to pay your expenses." I thanked him again for my liberty, and his good intentions towards me. I stayed with him until the monsoon; and during that time we made so many journeys to the hill that we filled all our warehouses with ivory. The other merchants who traded in it did the same thing, for it could not be long concealed from them.

The ships arrived at last, and my patron himself having made choice of the ship wherein I was to embark, he loaded half of it with ivory on my account, laid in provisions in abundance for my passage, and obliged me besides to accept as a present, curiosities of the country of great value. After I had returned him a thousand thanks for all his favours, I went on board. We set sail, and as the adventure which procured me this liberty was very extraordinary, I had it continually in my thoughts.

We stopped at some islands to take in fresh provisions. Our vessel being come to a port on the main land in the Indies, we touched there, and not being willing to venture by sea to Balsora, I landed my proportion of the ivory, resolving to proceed on my journey by land. I made vast sums by my ivory, I bought several rarities, which I intended for presents, and when my equipage was ready, I set out in the company of a large caravan of merchants. I was a long time on the way, and suffered very much, but endured all with patience, when I considered that I had nothing to fear from the seas, from pirates, from serpents, nor from the other perils I had undergone.

All these fatigues ended at last, and I came safe to Bagdad. I went immediately to wait upon the caliph, and gave him an account of my embassy. That prince told me he had been uneasy, by reason that I was so long in returning, but that he always hoped God would preserve me. When I told him the adventure of the elephants, he seemed to be much surprised at it, and would never have given any credit to it had he not known my sincerity. He reckoned this story, and the other narratives I had given him, to be so curious that he ordered one of his secretaries to write them in characters of gold, and lay them up in his treasury. I retired very well satisfied with the honours I received and the presents which he gave me; and after that I gave myself up wholly to my family, kindred and friends.